Bhagavad
Gita

薄伽梵歌

中英對照本

毗耶娑 | 著　周賓凰 | 譯

Content

〈專文推薦〉

「我所摯愛的……」

吳壽山

　　楊序指出了《薄伽梵歌》的哲學史話及修持指津，羅序也從佛法角度談到自證哲理、無我及二元論述，如果再加上譯者的導論，再回神看本書譯序，真是人生一大享受。

　　「當徒弟準備好時」，「師父」也「就會出現」了。依照這個語串，不論初讀或再閱修持，若能將導論與兩序連結合併，都慈悲地指向真理的精妙。因此，本書主張：只要學習如何超越造化三性，把身、口、意獻祭供養，反省本書梵歌七百句詩文，似如：來去人間鬧一鬧，更能捨棄無明與熱情，且臣服於上主，回到宇宙「無限的本質」。若論悅性、變性及惰性的正向力、反向力與中和力，乃進一步統整了人的個性與信仰；能有如此體驗，要感激上主的引導，譯者的用心與賢達的賜序。

　　佛緣人人有，哲理人人求，日本賢者稻盛和夫說：「做為人，何為正確？」，不但啟迪人心，也見到了「熱情」與「無明」，更參透了「純真」，對企業家精進在倫理與企業決策中，有如明燈。譯者於導論中，提出造化廿四締，更引出了「苦」、「集」、「滅」、「道」的架構，反向逐一的「捨棄」出離，也提出反思執著與認同，要能純真「臣服」，使個性及潛意識放下，皆臣服於專注上主。

　　平等看待好惡、成敗、榮辱等二元對立，從內在捨棄而不

執著，熱情無明皆能放心放下。譯者亦曾引以水入沙土為戒，歌詠水消失於沙土之後，風出尚能使水出，又入江河，結尾修持的力量有多大：藉著臣服於上主與捨棄，水終能匯入大海，成就無限的愛於上主之中。

感佩近十多年來，譯者的修持，已在本書中顯現出哲理（並於括弧中譯注），除了每頁下方的說明，值得一再返讀，每章詩文前的略語，也頗能了悟「哪有仇，哪有恨，皆土歸土，塵歸塵」。場域上的一切，實皆為造化之所為，譯者真誠反思，譯注出學習合一。

梵歌共有十八章的詩文，從閒雲野鶴的人看來，就是修持反省，可連結記憶，自然頓悟，說了熱情的累加，論了無明的活動，使人更易體會屬於聖靈的科學與自我的認識，也是藝術，也是聖典。

每天何妨一章？每月何妨一思？每年何妨一念？本書多語說詞，談出清晰，理出頭緒，皆是修持多元。享受靜默，信心不墜，總是滿足，不為喜怒畏懼所動，不期待什麼，無悲亦無求。譯者當已如是，且純真，理熱情，離無明。以此閱後心得代序，回應我所摯愛的……。

吳壽山識於八二三炮戰後六十年

（本文作者現為國立臺灣師範大學講座教授，曾任證券櫃檯買賣中心董事長、長庚大學管理學院院長、國立交通大學管理科學系所所長）

〈專文推薦〉

印度哲學及靈性修持的圭臬

楊台基

　　約莫三千五百年前，在現今的印度大地上發生了一場大戰，因著這場大戰，將當時邦國林立、常相爭戰的印度結合成一個大國。這場戰事的前前後後，由大哲毗耶娑以歷史演義的筆法寫成《摩訶婆羅多》一書傳世，成為史詩級的巨作。

　　《薄伽梵歌》的內容取自《摩訶婆羅多》第六章毗濕摩篇裡，克里希納對般度軍先發主將阿朱納的戰前開導。

　　《薄伽梵歌》最早的梵漢中譯本於一九五七年出版，譯者是赴印留學、有玄奘第二美稱的學者徐梵澄先生，自謂為其嘔心之作；為對應梵文典雅，採用的是騷體文筆法，頗具特色，然現代人讀之不易。再來是一九七〇年程兆熊博士以對偶句文體翻譯的《博伽梵曲》。其餘譯本，可參考本書導讀中的介紹。

　　克里希納在這場戰爭中的所為，後世評價兩極，但無疑的，是他決定了戰事的成敗，他是這場戰事的靈魂人物。事實上克里希納在加入戰役之前，已是傳奇人物。

　　襁褓時期的他逃過表舅坎薩的追殺，從秣菟羅逃到弗林達邦。自小即受到鄉親非常的喜愛，他的特質和笛聲能喚起聽者內心莫名的狂喜，故身邊不乏玩伴圍繞，咸認他是神的化身。有首詩是這麼形容他的：

「……克里希納帶來希望，克里希納就是希望，是庇護的希望、是解脫的希望。只要看到他一眼，就會為我們的心靈帶來平靜；他讓我們的雙眼多麼地快樂，讓我們的內心多麼地喜悅，……只要他甜美的微笑就夠讓我陶醉的了。」

克里希納少年中期告別了弗林達邦，回到秣菟羅，用計除掉了強大的暴君坎薩，被擁為王。當時的印度最大王國是摩揭陀，國王是克里希納的表兄，很敵視克里希納。在克里希納成為國君後，便經常藉故攻打秣菟羅。克里希納知道彼時無法力抗，便將首都從秣菟羅遠遷德瓦爾卡，一方面阻止攻擊，一方面積蓄實力。然後以法性號召盟友，終於打敗了摩揭陀，聲名遠播。

般度五子的母親是克里希納的姑姑，所以般度五子和克里希納是表兄弟關係；克里希納和阿朱納特別投緣，還將自己的妹妹嫁給阿朱納。俱盧族難敵百子是般度五子的堂兄弟，和克里希納算是遠親；然而克里希納的兒子娶了難敵的女兒，彼此又成了親家，其中俱有故事。般度、俱盧雙方交惡至不免一戰時，自然都想得到克里希納的支持。

於是克里希納邀約兩方表達意向。抵達時，克里希納正假寐中。難敵是國王身分，先被引進屋，入門後逕自坐到床首；阿朱納後進，選擇坐在床尾。因此克里希納醒來時眼光就先落在阿朱納身上：「喔，是你，阿朱納，歡迎，歡迎！很高興看到你。」之後轉頭看到難敵：「喔，難敵，你也來了，歡迎，歡迎！也很高興看到你。」

克里希納說你們來尋求我的支持，我有個想法，我和我的

軍隊，你們各擇其一；選我的人就不能選我的軍隊，選我的軍隊就不能選我。而且我不直接參戰，只幫忙駕馭戰車。結果阿朱納先選擇了克里希納，難敵也高興地選擇了克里希納強大的軍隊。這件插曲隱隱透露出克里希納對未來的大戰已然胸有成竹，盡在掌握之中。

開戰之前，兩軍陣列俱盧之野。阿朱納重情義，站在克里希納駕馭的戰車上，望向俱盧軍中曾經熟悉的親友，他看到他敬愛的舅公、更遠處的伯父，看到自己的業師德羅那、堂兄弟俱盧百子、同父異母的兄弟卡爾納及其他親友等等。思及即將掀起的殺戮與戰後巨大的影響和牽連，不禁悲從中來，鬥志全消。他質疑問道：

「即使擁有三界，我也不願殺他們，更何況是為此寂寥大地？這更有甚於戮及吾身。」

「我的主啊！持國王子嗣們的死亡能帶來什麼快樂呢？殺了這些險惡之徒，只是徒增罪孽罷了。……我們怎能由殺害親族而得到幸福呢？」（1:36-38）

意志消沉的阿朱納接連地舉問心中疑惑，克里希納則以永恆長明的角度次第破其盲點迷思。使阿朱納深深地瞭解到一切的源頭、一切的歸宿，以及生死之間存在的實義。其間克里希納更顯現出宇宙之主的本相！讓阿朱納見到一切他所認為如真的人、事、物，一切生、住、滅，都是宇宙之主的心靈投射；一切自祂而出，一切復歸於祂，真實不虛！

阿朱納啊！且看那整個寰宇，不論是會動或不會動的事物，以及任何你想看到的東西；所有一切全都活在我之內，成為一體。（11:7）

克里希納這番盡除阿朱納胸中疑惑、使他重拾戰鬥意志的開示，大哲毗耶娑將之為文記下，展現於世。緣克里希納本相是宇宙之主，換言之，《薄伽梵歌》就是「擁有上主特質之人的說法」；由於其深邃的內容，開啟了讀者精神的新視界，公認是印度哲學及靈性修持的圭臬。

摩訶婆羅多之戰裡，克里希納的作為令很多人不解。事實上，即便在那時，也少有人瞭解克里希納的真實身分，但是通過《薄伽梵歌》的流傳，讓讀者認識到真正的克里希納和他的所為及宏圖偉略。如《薄伽梵歌》所說：

「每當靈性衰退、物欲橫行，阿朱納啊，我就會轉世降生。」（4:7）
「阿朱納啊！我知曉過去、現在、未來一切之眾生，但他們並不認識我。」（7:26）

摩訶婆羅多戰事已遠，但留存下來的故事和教誨不受時空侷限地代代綿延。若說俱盧之地象徵著所處的世界，法性之地暗喻著我們的身體；持國王是盲目的心靈，般度五子代表著人身的五個脈輪，俱盧百子代表著種種的習性，那麼這場戰爭就轉而成為過去、現在、未來每個人的戰爭。而《薄伽梵歌》將

是使我們從這場戰事中勝出的指津。

（本文作者為阿南達瑪迦瑜伽靜坐協會創會理事長，修行瑜伽
靜坐斷食四十餘年）

〈專文推薦〉

《薄伽梵歌》是不可不讀的文獻

羅卓仁謙

　　從佛法研究者的角度來看，印度教與佛法的關係實在是你中有我、我中有你；印度教認為佛陀是毗濕奴神的化身，佛法認為梵天、因陀羅等印度教大神是佛陀的支持者。從哲理上的發展來看更是如此：在公元前五世紀左右興起的沙門主義中，包括佛法、耆那教等思想代表著衝撞著傳統婆羅門體制的新興思潮，這不但讓印度文化圈出現了截然不同的思想體系，同時也讓婆羅門教本身開始出現改革。

　　佛滅後，婆羅門教開始出現更多與宗教分離、偏向純哲學性的著作。當然，在婆羅門教的體制下，仍然不會逾越吠陀主義、梵我主義的思潮。其中最為著名的代表作之一，就是《薄伽梵歌》。

　　這部著作的價值與重要性，在譯者寫的導讀與譯序中已經深入淺出地有所介紹，我就不拾人牙慧；從另一個比較少人切入的角度來談談《薄伽梵歌》的重要性，也就是其對佛法的影響。

一、哲學化

　　時至今日，許多人認為佛法屬於「哲學」。但如果單純以原始佛法為例，相對於哲學，毋寧說其更帶有認知學、甚至於

科學的特色，關鍵原因在於佛陀本人在原始佛法聖典中，對形而上的哲學問題採取不回應──也就是「無記」的態度；更有甚者，佛陀極為重視「可驗證」這個科學特性，佛法專有名詞稱為「自證」。

然而，在佛滅後，以《薄伽梵歌》為首的印度的吠檀多哲學之興起，在很大的程度上衝擊了佛法，甚至可以說讓佛法內部產生改革與思維，很大層面地豐富了佛法理論；當然這樣的層面也影響了後世受佛法影響的中國哲學、西藏哲學等。因此，我們甚至可以說：《薄伽梵歌》對佛法、對其餘地區的哲學影響是深入而廣泛的。

二、無我

早在奧義書時代，吠陀主義就已經對於至高至上的靈魂──梵我──作出哲學上的詮釋，從否定面、其超越思議的面向來詮釋其功德；而在梵書中則提到更多其正面、肯定的優點。這些特質在《薄伽梵歌》中有一統性的解釋。許多人以為，「無我」是佛法獨有的理論，其實不然，吠陀主義也闡述某種「無我」：無小我而有大我，此大我即是梵我。但梵我對於一般人來說，實在太難體悟與經驗了，唯有透過虔敬這條道路可以抵達。這樣的論點不但在《薄伽梵歌》中表露無遺，甚至也影響了後代佛法的如來藏思想，《寶性論》中就強調想要體悟如來藏的人必須：「唯依如來信，信於第一義，如無眼目者，不能見日輪。」

如來藏思想是大乘佛法、甚至密乘佛法的核心，在是否受

到印度梵我思想影響的論戰上，大家一向莫衷一是；但我更相信，要知道這個論調是不是來自梵我、與梵我的關係，那我們務必得去認識「梵我」本身長什麼樣子，而詮釋其特質最為完整的著作，不外就是《薄伽梵歌》。

三、二元論

　　《薄伽梵歌》受數論派哲學影響，表現出強烈的二元論：物質與精神的對立，這種思想根本上影響了佛法——特別是大乘佛法！不論是其「微塵」的論調對小乘宗派所主張「無方極微塵」的影響，或是大乘每每都將「能所」、「心物」、「境有境」這一組一組的主觀與客觀視為對立，都能隱約看到二元論的影子；特別是精神原始無誤、出現錯誤後而投射出整個世界，更有明顯的數論派哲學味道；而若要對這樣的論述源頭有更清楚的認識，那《薄伽梵歌》更是不可不讀的文獻。

　　《薄伽梵歌》本來是以嚴謹的詩歌體呈現，深澀而難懂；但這次的《薄伽梵歌》譯本，相較之下好讀又忠於原文，實為華人讀者之福！希望類似著作的整理與翻譯，能夠讓華人社會可以更全面地瞭解印度各派哲學中，互相影響的關係與痕跡。

（本文作者為九〇後，熟悉漢、藏、梵、英四語的佛學學者）

〈譯序〉

關於《薄伽梵歌》的二三事

　　1943 年，當世界第一顆原子彈在德州的沙漠上空引爆，發出耀目閃光、冒起巨型蘑菇狀雲時，目睹原子彈爆炸威力的歐本海默（Robert Oppenheimer，原子彈之父）腦中浮現的是《薄伽梵歌》中，克里希納的毀滅者形象：「現在我成了死神，世界的毀滅者。」他所描繪的，是克里希納揭示給阿朱納王子的靈視景象——克里希納的毀滅者形象，遠超過我們對「天地不仁，以萬物為芻狗」的想像。

　　時間鏡頭往後拉到 1948 年 1 月 30 日，當一位印度教狂熱分子朝著甘地的胸膛開槍時，甘地才剛結束生平的第 14 次絕食，正徒步前往道場準備為信眾講述《薄伽梵歌》。生後，他的財產也就只有幾枝筆、幾件衣服與一本《薄伽梵歌》。甘地一生信奉的非暴力與公民不服從運動，係受到梭羅的啟發，而梭羅的理念正是來自《薄伽梵歌》。甘地的信念推動了印度的獨立，又啟發了後來馬丁路德‧金與曼德拉的民主運動。

　　東方的思想傳到西方，經過一番淬鍊又從西方回到東方；然後在印度開花後，同樣的種子又再度飄向西方。

　　在學術界，著名的生物學與博物學家威爾森（Edward Wilson）在他的鉅著《社會生物學》（*Sociobiology*; 1975）中，結合了社會學與生物學探討生物界的演化。然而在書的開

頭，他引用《薄伽梵歌》中的句子：「聖靈既不殺，也不被殺。」（2:19）因為在這看似弱肉強食的造化背後，還有一個更大的力量：是聖靈、是上帝、是自性（佛性），那是所有想要「回家」的人尋找的地方。

著名的修行者自傳《瑜伽之龍》（*Autobiography of a Yogi*）作者尤伽南達（Paramahansa Yogananda）說克里希納是誕生在印度的基督，而《薄伽梵歌》正是印度教的聖經、福音書。

❋

在華人世界裡，《薄伽梵歌》是一部被長久忽視的經典。不論宗教信仰為何，一般人都知道《聖經》是基督教的經典，《阿彌陀經》、《心經》是佛教的經典，甚至《可蘭經》，很多人也都知道它是伊斯蘭教（回教）的經典；但印度教及其經典（包括《薄伽梵歌》）對多數華人而言，卻是全然地陌生。

印度人口約 12 億，其中印度教徒占八成，如果加上散布在其他國家的印度教徒，全球大概有 10 億人是信奉印度教的；以信徒人數而言，印度教僅次於基督宗教與伊斯蘭教，還遠高於佛教，是世界第三大宗教。

事實上，《薄伽梵歌》作為印度教三大聖典之一，自十七世紀被帶到西方社會（很諷刺的是，宗教竟然常是隨著經濟或武力的「暴力」而傳播的），至今光是英文譯本就已經數百種，足見其在西方人士心中的重要地位。相較之下，中文譯本則只有寥寥五、六種，實在是少得可憐。我們對印度教的陌生，有點令人納悶。尤其是佛教也是源自印度，但卻能在東方扎根茁壯；而同樣源自印度的印度教，似乎就硬生生地被擋在

喜馬拉雅山以南了。或許是因為中國佛教早期動輒把其他宗教斥為「外道」？又或許是因為佛教是「無神論」，而印度教是有神祇信仰的？

《薄伽梵歌》一直以來是屬於小眾的書，僅在一些慕道友間流傳。十多年前剛接觸到這本經典時，第一個印象是很訝異這樣一部重要的經典，竟然只有短短七百句詩文（頌）！當時心態上只是把它當作又一本的靈修書，所以很快就讀完一遍；雖然覺得「書」中有些不錯的觀點，但更覺得很多地方艱澀難解。於是把找得到的中文譯本都看過，不同譯文的差異反而讓我更困惑，所以也就把它放在一邊。

直到幾年前（2011）從書架上把幾本《薄伽梵歌》中譯本又拿下來讀，發現仍有許多地方不甚瞭解，才想到為何不看看英文的譯本？網路一搜尋，才赫然發現這部經書竟然有這麼多的英譯本；而仔細研讀，比較對照了幾個譯本，原本許多不清楚的地方也就慢慢地釐清了。因為有了一點點的心得，所以也就突發奇想（願）：何不把這些心得整理出來！

這譯本就是這個「願」的結果。開始《薄伽梵歌》的翻譯到初稿完成，只花了一個月，但之後的幾年經過數十次的修改；每次的修訂總為我帶來一些不同的體會。反覆研讀的過程中，我深深感受到這是值得、也需要以虔誠的心來誦讀的一部經典。這譯本當然不會是最好的中譯本，我僅僅希望這樣一部珍貴的神聖經典可以讓更多人認識。不過受限於個人的資質，譯文不免會有失真之處。如果讀者發現謬誤不清之處，尚請勞煩告知。

與以往的中譯本有些不一樣的地方。首先是我採用了中英對照，如此當讀者對中文有疑慮時，可就英文譯文再做釐清。第二，我雖然是以普羅希（Shri Purohit Swami, 1935）的英譯為主，但也就其他不同英譯本做了一些補充。普羅希（1882-1941）生於印度，於 1930 年在他的古魯（靈性導師）的指引下來到歐洲，是近代將印度宗教思想帶到西方的幾位瑜伽修行者之一。他的主要貢獻之一就是翻譯了《薄伽梵歌》，也與著名的愛爾蘭詩人葉慈一起翻譯主要的幾本《奧義書》。普羅希的譯文相當精簡，而其中有一特色就是以意譯為主，並以較有基督宗教意味的詞彙來詮釋許多印度教的專有詞彙，因而更易於被歐美人士接受。我在這個版本中，也就原本的印度教詞彙與相關背景知識做了一些補充。

第三，由於《薄伽梵歌》中有很多內容涉及印度的哲學思想，對多數的中文讀者來說是陌生的，因此我在譯文前增添了〈導讀〉；就一些背景資料做補充。另一個與過去譯本不同的是，我也嘗試以較現代的語彙——包括從心理學的觀點——來闡釋《薄伽梵歌》的一些意涵。希望對讀者在研讀《薄伽梵歌》時，能有些助益。

最後，我覺得《薄伽梵歌》不僅是一部引導我們人生方向的偉大經典，更是一本福音書，因為克里希納在《薄伽梵歌》中說：

「每當靈性衰退、物欲橫行……我就會轉世降生！」

　　上主並不唯獨在印度示現，也不唯獨以克里希納、老子、耶穌或穆罕默德的形象出現。但我們怎麼認出祂呢？有一句諺語是這麼說的：

「當徒弟準備好時，師父就會出現。」

　　對我而言，師父早就出現了，而且也一直很慈悲地在等待我準備好。

謹識於 2018 年 6 月

〈導讀〉

一場奇妙而不可思議的對話

　　印度是許多宗教的發源地，而這些宗教的源頭又可回溯到印度教。大概是出於這樣的原因，著名的宗教學大師休斯頓·史密斯（Huston Smith）在他的《世界宗教》（*The World's Religions*, 1995），就是以印度教作為開頭的。

　　印度教三大聖典之一的《薄伽梵歌》（*Bhagavad Gita*，簡稱《梵歌》），意為上主之歌（The Song of God），係記載上主師利克里希納（Lord Shri Krishna）與阿朱納（Arjuna）王子間一場奇妙而不可思議的對話。[1] 歷來《薄伽梵歌》被尊為是最重要的印度教修行聖典，同時也是許多印度大修行者最重視的經典，對今日之印度乃至全世界的很多層面，都有著極大的影響。聖雄甘地在他的自傳中說：「真理是至高的原則，而《薄伽梵歌》乃是指向真理之知識中，最精妙的書。」（見史密斯，1995）。[2]

1　另兩部則是《吠陀》（*Vedas*）與《奧義書》（*Upanishads*）。不過《吠陀》與《奧義書》都不是單一的經典，而是許多經典的集合，內容遍及宗教、文學、詩歌等。同時，「奧義書」也廣泛地被視為是印度經典的代表，例如，《薄伽梵歌》每章的結尾都稱其為奧義書之一。

2　就政治而言，眾所皆知印度與巴基斯坦是在聖雄甘地的領導下獨立建國的；甘地「非暴力不合作主義」（Satyagraha）的提出是受到梭羅（Henry David Thoreau）的「公民不服從」（Civil Disobedience）的啟發，而梭羅則是受到《薄伽梵歌》的啟迪。美國馬丁路德·金博士與南非曼德拉則又是受到甘地的影響。近年來為世界之永續未來而發展出來的綠色經濟學，其在地化（localization）、自力更生（self reliance）等觀念，也受到甘

「薄伽梵」中譯為上主或上帝，在印度的靈性傳承裡，代表的是上帝在地球上的化身（avatar），相當於猶太教與基督宗教中的彌賽亞（救世主）。在早期的佛教經典中，薄伽梵與佛（buddha）是同義字。例如，玄奘法師的《金剛經》譯本中，就依照梵文原文，將佛陀直譯為薄伽梵。其實佛經中，徒弟稱呼釋迦牟尼佛為世尊（Lord），事實上也就是上主之意。如今的印度教把釋迦牟尼佛尊為毗濕奴（Vishnu、Mahavisnu）的第九個化身，而史詩《羅摩衍那》（*Ramayana*）中羅摩王與《薄伽梵歌》中的克里希納則分別是其第七與第八個化身。[3] 不論是耶穌、克里希納，或釋迦牟尼佛，在經典中，徒弟們也都稱祂們為師父（Master），可見祂們都是了悟上帝（或者說是阿耨多羅三邈三菩提）的在世明師（living masters），以內在與外在的教理教導徒弟了悟自性（Self、atman），也就是重新與上帝合一；只是因為文化上的歧異，以及徒弟與後世信徒的理解不同，而衍生出後來種種不同的宗教與派別。

　　《薄伽梵歌》出自史詩《摩訶婆羅多》（*Mahabharata*）的第六篇〈毗濕摩〉篇；全書十八章，總共只有 700 行詩句（也稱「頌」）。[4]《摩訶婆羅多》全詩計有十八篇，長達十萬頌，是《依里亞得》（*Iliad*）與《奧德賽》（*Odyssey*）合起來的七倍長、聖經長度的三倍，據稱是現今世界上最長的史詩（Fosse，

地影響甚多（見 Cato，2010 ）。

3　毗濕奴原為印度婆羅門教中的三大主神之一，另兩位是梵天（Brahma）與濕婆（Shiva），但毗濕奴後來演變成為代表一切的首位大神。

4　頌是古印度文的詩體單位，每頌兩行 32 個音節。

2007）；[5]《摩訶婆羅多》與《羅摩衍那》為印度的兩大史詩，後者的長度僅為前者的四分之一。[6]《摩訶婆羅多》的作者據說是毗耶娑（Vyasa，也譯廣博仙人；毗耶娑也有編撰者的意思），但現今歷史學家多認為不是一人於一時一地所做，最初大概是由遊方僧侶以口述的方式流傳，之後再經歷代編撰而成的。

《摩訶婆羅多》敘述俱盧族的持國王（Dhritarashtra）百子與般度（Pandu）五子，雙方陣營為爭奪王權而進行的一場戰爭。這場戰爭雖然僅僅進行了十八天，但戰況卻是慘烈異常，雙方幾乎全數陣亡；最後僅有般度五子與其他少數幾個人存活下來，贏得最後的勝利。

很多人在研讀《薄伽梵歌》時，對於其中似乎支持戰爭的論點而感到很不自在；對於相信眾生原是一體而倡導「非暴力」（ahimsa、non-violence）的人（尤其是佛教徒與耆那教徒）而言，更是如此，因為戰爭與非暴力根本就是南轅北轍的兩回事。不過印度聖雄甘地所倡導的非暴力運動，其思想源頭正是《薄伽梵歌》。同樣的一部經典，為什麼傳達出來的觀點會是如此衝突呢？甘地認為，如果人僅僅因為《薄伽梵歌》所描述的戰爭背景，就認為《薄伽梵歌》允許暴力，那是對《薄伽梵歌》的斷章取義——他很難想像一個人怎麼可能既遵循《薄伽梵歌》的教誨，而又能服從於暴力。

----

5 另一說法是《摩訶婆羅多》計有74000頌，加上一些不同語體的散文句。
6 黃寶生（2005）等人所譯的《摩訶婆羅多》中文譯本，長達五百萬字，共六大冊。另外，有關兩大史詩的介紹，可參考江亦麗（2007）、夏塔克（C. Shattuck, 1999）《印度教的世界》，與黃晨淳編著（2004）的《印度神話故事》。《摩訶婆羅多》的故事亦可參考林懷民（2008）譯自卡里耶爾的法文劇本，黃寶生（2005）的《摩訶婆羅多導讀》，或是維基百科中的介紹。

關於這個問題，埃克納斯·伊斯瓦蘭（Eknath Easwaran, 1985）指出兩個不同的既存觀點：第一個看法是，《薄伽梵歌》是允許戰爭的——如果戰爭是為了正當或正義的理由；第二個看法是，有些人認為《摩訶婆羅多》，尤其是《薄伽梵歌》，徹頭徹尾談的都是人內在的戰爭，特別是修行人在靈修過程中所遇到的各種內在衝突與掙扎，所以並不是發生在現實世界的實際戰事。不過近年來卻有些考古學上的發現，證明《摩訶婆羅多》敘述的戰事似乎確有其事。

其實《薄伽梵歌》說得很清楚：我們每個人都受到造化三性中所主導的力量的影響，因此對同一事物也會有不同的理解；即使是同一個人，在不同的時空下，觀念也可能會有所不同，一個絕對正確的單一觀點並不存在。[7] 毫無疑問地，克里希納在《薄伽梵歌》中所揭示的一個重要啟示，是要我們學習超越造化三性，把所有的身口意都視為是對上主的獻祭供養。

背景概述

如前所說的，《摩訶婆羅多》敘述俱盧族的持國王百子與般度五子間的故事。在《摩訶婆羅多》中，般度諸子代表「正義」的一方，而持國子嗣則是「邪惡」的一方（他們的關係，請見下圖）。持國與般度是兄弟，分別由兩位王后所生，其親生父親則是毗耶娑（廣博仙人）。[8] 由於持國生而眼盲，因

---

7 關於造化三性，請見稍後的說明。
8 這裡關係有點複雜。持國百子與般度五子的曾祖父福身王（Shantanu）與恆河女神（Ganga）生下毗濕摩（Bhishma），與貞信（Satyavati）也生下兩子，分別是花

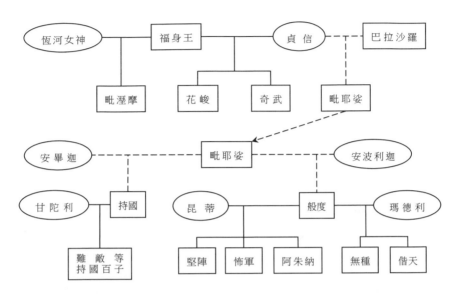

此由其弟般度擔任象城的國王。後來般度王在打獵時誤殺仙人，遭受詛咒，因而把王位讓給持國，並與其兩位王后——昆蒂（Kunti）與瑪德利（Madri）自我放逐。般度的兩位王后先後生下五個兒子，即「般度五子」：堅陣（Yudishthira）、怖軍（Bhima）、阿朱納（Arjuna，亦譯「有修」）、無種（Nakula）與偕天（Sahadeva）。[9] 後來般度逝世，王后昆蒂於是把年幼的

峻（Chitrangada）與奇武（Vichitravirya），但兩子在繼任王位後皆早死，沒有留下子嗣。毗濕摩因對父親的承諾，一生未婚，也不願繼承王位，在幾代間一直扮演著相當於攝政王的角色。為了王國子嗣的延續，太后貞信於是召請毗耶娑與奇武的兩位王后——安畢迦（Ambika）與安波利迦（Ambalika）結婚，分別生下持國與般度。毗耶娑雖是持國與般度的生父，但並不是王族成員，而是太后貞信在與福身王結婚前與遊方修士巴拉沙羅所生。毗濕摩是持國與般度的伯父，也是故事中整個家族中最年長的。相關人物的關係，請見上方圖表（參考黃晨淳〔2004〕與 Yogananda〔1999〕）。

9 在史詩中，般度五子是昆蒂和瑪德利與不同的天神所生的。關於這點有兩種不同看法：一是認為「與神所生」並不是肉身上的意涵；另一是認為當時沒有嚴格的社會制度，甚至是母系社會為主流，因此堅陣等人有可能非般度親生的。

五子帶回象城，與持國王的一百個兒子（即「持國百子」，以
長子難敵〔Duryodhana〕為首[10]）一起長大，也一同向德羅那學
習武藝。[11]

　　但這群堂兄弟的相處是很不融洽的，彼此間的衝突不斷；
般度五子的武藝與學習都相當傑出，品行也良好。這引起了難
敵兄弟們的忌妒與怨恨，害怕般度諸子會自他們的父親手中奪
走王位。事實上，持國王心中也多有掙扎：他一方面認為應把
王位交還給堅陣，但另一方面也受不了難敵的慫恿，想把王位
留給自己的兒子。

　　就在難敵的設計陷害下，般度五子與母親昆蒂差點陷身
火窟，因而走上逃亡流浪之路。稍後，在木柱王為女兒德羅帕
蒂（Draupadi，也譯「黑公主」）的比武招親大會上，阿朱納以
其神射手的精湛武藝贏得比賽，並依昆蒂的要求，五位兄弟合
娶了德羅帕蒂為妻。

　　由於般度五子與木柱王的這層關係，儘管有著難敵的阻
擋，持國王仍接受了毗濕摩與德羅那的建議，認為般度五子也
有繼承王國的權利，因而將一半的王國分給般度五子統治。就
在四位兄弟的輔佐下，堅陣王把國家治理得井然有序、富強繁

---

10 根據《摩訶婆羅多》，甘陀利王后原來是生了一個肉球；肉球後來被剖成一百塊，灑上聖
　水後才變成持國百子。有一個解釋是眼盲的持國王象徵我們盲目的心靈，而持國百子則是
　我們身體的各種作用、習性。參見雪莉·雪莉·阿南達慕提（2008，第92頁）。
11 般度五子與持國百子同屬俱盧族，但一般為區分方便，都稱般度五子一方為般度族，而
　持國百子一方為俱盧族。另外，昆蒂與克里希納同屬雅度族，所以般度五子與克里希納
　在血緣上，是表兄弟的關係。稍晚在般度諸子遭放逐的十三年間，阿朱納也娶了克里希
　納的妹妹妙賢（Subhadra；也譯「善賢」）為妻；所以，阿朱納也是克里希納的妹婿。
　阿朱納與妙賢生有一子，名為激昂（Abhimanyu）。激昂在俱盧之戰中也陣亡，他的兒
　子環住則在多年後繼任堅陣為王。

榮，鄰國也紛紛向他們稱臣納貢。這就又引起了難敵的憤慨，於是設局邀請堅陣賭骰子。儘管其他兄弟阻撓，堅陣卻對賭骰子完全沒有抗拒的能力。果然在難敵的詭計下，堅陣一路賭輸：首飾、大量的黃金、僕役、戰馬、牛隊、羊群，最後連王國、自己、兄弟、孩子與德羅帕蒂，都輸給了難敵。般度五子受到了難敵的刁難、侮辱，直到持國王終於看不下去而出面主持正義，要求難敵將贏來的一切還給堅陣。

由於擔心堅陣兄弟的報復，難敵邀堅陣再賭最後的一局：輸者必須流放森林十二年，並在第十三年隱姓埋名，不被人認出，否則就須再流放十二年。歷史果然重演，堅陣輸了最後的一局。堅陣懊悔不已，但他的兄弟們與德羅帕蒂仍堅定地加入了他放逐的行列。

漫長的十三年終於熬過去，般度五子表明身分，並向難敵要求歸還國土，但雙方談判破裂；難敵甚至連五個村莊、五間房子也不願給予──雙方的戰爭變得不可避免。般度五子有木柱王（德羅帕蒂之父）以及摩差國（般度五子第十三年所待的國家）的加入，以怖軍為主帥；難敵等持國百子的俱盧族則以毗濕摩為主帥。克里希納以人類形象降生在雅度族，在這場戰爭中擔任阿朱納王子的馭者，為他駕馭戰車。

戰爭在俱盧之野進行。由於持國王眼不能視，毗耶娑願意賜給他視力，讓他看到戰爭的情況。但持國王不忍親眼看到親族間的殺戮，毗耶娑遂將靈視的力量賜予他的大臣山佳亞（Sanjaya，亦譯「良知」、「全勝」），由山佳亞為持國王轉述戰況。《薄伽梵歌》就是開戰前，克里希納與阿朱納王子間的

一場靈性對話，藉由山佳亞之口說與持國王聆聽。

在這場對話之後，接著的就是為期十八天的戰爭，戰況空前激烈，屍橫遍野，雙方的死傷都非常慘重。難敵一方全部罹難，包括毗濕摩、德羅那、持國百子等人，而般度一方也幾乎只剩下般度五子存活。史詩《摩訶婆羅多》最後一篇〈升天篇〉敘述堅陣繼任王位，統治三十六年後，將王位傳給孫子（激昂之子環住王）。兄弟五人與德羅帕蒂前往雪山（喜馬拉雅山）朝覲。途中德羅帕蒂與阿朱納等人相繼死亡，最後只有堅陣與陪伴他的一隻狗到達天堂之門。

令堅陣驚訝的是，難敵等兄弟竟然已在天堂享樂，而他的兄弟卻是在地獄受苦。隨後雷神因陀羅（Indra）揭示這種種一切原是幻象。堅陣終於了悟，超越了一切仇恨與煩惱，與他的兄弟等人一起進入了天堂，並瞭解到原來他的兄弟與許多的戰士們原就是天神的化身。

※

《摩訶婆羅多》中所敘述的戰事發生於何時，乃至成書的日期，已很難確認。從靈性的角度來看，時間正如物質般地同等虛幻，這大概也是何以早期的印度與中國哲學（像是印度教與老莊思想等）都很難確認其歷史的年代（甚且連作者都不詳）。雖然考證探究這些歷史真相不是本書的目的，但似乎還是有必要簡短交代一下相關的歷史。

大致上，西方學者的考證多認定此一史詩大概完成於西元前二世紀到西元後二世紀之間（或說是西元前後四世紀之間），認為其思想受到佛教、耆那教、數論等影響。這一派看法之所

以認為《薄伽梵歌》晚於佛教等宗教的原因之一，是因為主要的佛教經典（約完成於西元前五、六世紀間）皆未提及《薄伽梵歌》中的相關人物或思想。此外，不論是《摩訶婆羅多》或是《羅摩衍那》，都被認為一開始是以口語相傳的形式流傳，之後再經過世世代代增刪編撰而有今日之面貌；甚至有人認為《薄伽梵歌》是後來才被安插到《摩訶婆羅多》的內文之中。至於印度的相關論述，則都傾向於把史詩的年代拉到遠古以前（西元前 3102 年），以「證明」印度教的起源早於所有其他宗教。[12]

英文版本說明

《薄伽梵歌》最早的英譯本是由查爾斯·威爾金斯（Charles Wilkins）於 1785 年所譯；有人統計，早在 1980 年代初期就已經有超過四十種英文譯本。[13] 如今《薄伽梵歌》已被翻譯成各種文字，光是英文版本就已超過數百種。

相對之下，中文的譯本似乎就有點少了。目前中譯本裡，從梵文直接翻譯的，如黃寶生（2005）、邱顯峰（2010）、鍾文秀（2011），也有從英文版翻譯而來的，如楊斐華（1985，根據普羅希的英譯）、懷塵（1999，根據希瓦南達（Sivananda）的英譯）。由於每位譯者的學思背景各不相同，所以也很難說哪一

---

12 參閱維基百科 http://en.wikipedia.org/wiki/Bhagavad_Gita 或是 Srimad Bhagavad Gita 中的介紹（http://www.bhagavad-gita.org/Gita/intro.html）。

13 近代印度思想傳至西方，尤其是在靈性的傳承方面，與帝國主義時期英國東印度公司的入侵殖民印度有很大的關係，威爾金斯即受雇於當時的英屬東印度公司。有關《薄伽梵歌》流通歷史的簡介，也可參閱 http://en.wikipedia.org/wiki/Bhagavad_Gita。

個版本較貼近原意，更何況讀者的認知、背景也有所歧異，因此所好也各有不同。

的確，就如《薄伽梵歌》所揭示的：我們每個人都受到造化三性中所主導之力量的影響。因此我們每個人也都以其獨特的方式來解讀——或說是「編碼」（coding）——這個世界；即便是同樣一句話，在每個人心中所傳達的意念、印象也都不同。所以，誠如一位讀者在亞馬遜網路書店上對各種《薄伽梵歌》版本所作的評論：完美的版本並不存在。

休斯頓·史密斯在他的《世界宗教》一書中提到，在伊斯蘭教穆斯林的眼中，《可蘭經》被視為是「非創造的《可蘭經》」（Uncreated Koran）的塵世摹本，前者——也就是「創造的《可蘭經》」（Created Koran）——是後者的無限本質透過文字與聲音具體化呈現的。在許多人（尤其是印度教徒）的心中，《薄伽梵歌》所記載的，一如基督徒眼中的《聖經》一樣，正是上帝的話語。只是當上帝的無限本質以有限的物質造化方式來表達時，必然無法完全完美地呈現或被瞭解。

這個中英對照版本以普羅希的英譯為主，也參考了伊斯瓦蘭、福斯（Lars M. Fosse）、甘地、希瓦南達、尤迦南達等人的英譯本。譯者認為普羅希的英譯有幾個特色：

一、他的英文簡明，很多地方頗有《聖經》、《道德經》與佛經的簡單美。

二、在翻譯上，很多地方是意譯的，尤其是當一些內容牽涉到印度教的文化背景或一些專有名詞時。譯者對這樣的作法頗為贊同，畢竟對不熟悉印度文化的人而言，更重要的是《薄

伽梵歌》中所傳達的主要訊息。

肯恩・威爾伯（Ken Wilber）認為在眾多英文譯本中，普羅希的英譯對於首次接觸《薄伽梵歌》的人，是最佳的版本。不過對於想要對印度文化有多一些認識的人，免不了會有一些失望。

正如許多譯者都會遭遇到的問題：很多的梵文名詞並沒有絕對的英文對應用詞，所以只要是翻譯，難免會有些「失真」。失真的來源是多重的：翻譯者對原文的理解、譯文的造詣等等。張澄基（1973）在談論一般人所困擾的佛教「無我論」時指出，因為梵文和巴利文類似中文沒有標點符號的習慣，也都沒有大寫小寫之分，因此比較容易造成混淆。例如，梵文中的「我」是 "ātman"。以英文用法而言，小寫就代表經驗的小我，而大寫則代表遍滿一切與宇宙合一的大我。由於梵文並無大小寫之分，因此容易變得義理不明，形成哲理上的爭執，甚至分裂成不同的流派。由於譯者是從英譯本再翻譯為中文，恐怕失真的程度更大。[14]

此外，很多詞彙一直都沒有統一的中文翻譯。例如，有人將「Self」與「self」分別譯為「大我」與「小我」，也有人將 Self 譯為「自性」、「自我」，或甚至是「本我」。另外，像是英文 mind 有時翻成「心」、「意念」、有時是「心智」，有時又可譯為「頭腦」。這些不同名詞在人們的心中，也都有不同的含

14《奇蹟課程》說：「文字不過是象徵（符號）的象徵，雙重地脫離了實相。」（Words are but symbols of symbols, twice removed from reality.）因為各靈性傳承都認為這個世界的本質是幻象（maya, illusion），而非實相；所以本質上，世界就是一堆符號（象徵）的組成，而文字則是彼此隔離的個體為溝通而發展出來描述這個世界的另一層「符號」，因此更是偏離了實相。這本中譯本是由梵轉英，再轉中，可見是「四重」地偏離實相。

意，因此在翻譯過程中，常常需斟酌哪一個詞彙是比較適合的。這也正是譯者在這個譯本中，以中英對照的方式呈現的主要原因；希望讀者在遇到譯文不通順時，可就英文原譯對照比較一番。雖說如此，譯者仍衷心希望能傳達出《薄伽梵歌》所要傳達的主要訊息。

在英譯部分，譯者參考柏洛茲（K. C. Burroughs, 2011）的作法，將一些較「古」的用字，像是 thou 與 thyself，換成現代的用字，也就是 you 與 yourself。另外，有些名詞也附上了其原有梵文的英文音譯，並就譯者有限的知識做了些微的補充。附帶一提，由於《薄伽梵歌》是從《摩訶婆羅多》中獨立出來的，原先每章並沒有標題；現行的標題都是後來翻譯者增添的，因此不同版本的標題也都各有歧異。例如，普羅希第一章的標題是「阿朱納的消沉意志」，但伊斯瓦蘭版本則是「內在的戰爭」（War Within），強調《薄伽梵歌》中所談論的，或者說其真正想表達的意義，是內在的征戰。尤迦南達就認為整部《薄伽梵歌》談論的，就是修行靜坐的體驗，因此也應由此觀點來頌持這部經典。

印度靈性思想的補充說明

印度的靈性思想久遠而繁複，想要有系統性、全面的瞭解，頗不容易。除了像是佛教因為流傳至中土甚早，有系統性的翻譯與整理外，其餘的靈性傳承，像是婆羅門教（乃至後來的印度教）、耆那教、錫克教等，都被視為是「外道」，因而不能有較

客觀的對待。以印度教思想而言，由於沒有「官方」的統一翻譯，又加上學者、譯者的背景與瞭解各有不同，所以許多印度教思想、詞彙的中譯都頗有歧異。有些對印度思想不甚瞭解（或不認同）的作者，甚至把各種印度教史詩與經書，視為是虛幻的神話故事，以狹隘的觀點來詮釋。在這一節裡，我們將就幾個與《薄伽梵歌》有關的主題，做一些說明。

《薄伽梵歌》與數論

數論（Samkhya）是印度正統哲學思想的六派之一，其創始人據傳是迦毘羅仙人（Sage Kapila），而其年代甚至也比一些奧義書還早。然而就如同許多古代中國哲學作品是後人假借古人之名而做，同樣也沒有任何證據證明數論為迦毘羅所作。由於《薄伽梵歌》中有多處論及數論，因此在這一節中，我們就數論的主要觀點做一些補充。[15]

菩盧薩與普拉克里提

儘管有人認為數論是印度帶給世人的最重要哲學體系，但今日人們對數論的解釋卻多有不同，迄今爭論仍未止息。這個結果並不令人驚訝，因為我們每個人原本就是以其獨特

---

15 數論在印度教中的角色相當於佛教中的唯識論，不過就譯者所知，數論的中文資料並不多，甚至連一本專著也沒有。多數的論著都是從哲學的角度談論，從靈性角度去談的則更少。近代密意主義「第四道」的創始人葛吉夫（Gurdjieff）對數論與印度思想有不少論述。葛吉夫以當代的語言，詮釋各種大至宇宙、小至個人的哲學，並主張兼容羯磨瑜伽、闍那瑜伽，與巴克提瑜伽的第四條道路，其中有頗多論述跟數論與《薄伽梵歌》的觀點相似。有興趣的讀者可參考鄔斯賓斯基所著的《第四道》與《探索奇蹟》二書（二書分別由斐華出版社與方智出版社出版）。

的方式認知這個世界,所以很自然地對事物的理解也必然不盡相同。例如,很多關於數論的哲學討論著重於其是否為「二元論」(dualism)。事實上,較原始版本的數論認為「菩盧薩」(Purusha、Purusa,一譯「補盧沙」)與「普拉克里提」(Prakriti)是組成宇宙的兩項元素,其中普拉克里提是「未顯」(unmanifest)、原初物質、所有物質與能量的總合,而菩盧薩則是神性的自我(神我),是純然意識,或者是個體性的「靈魂」。[16] 宇宙的演化是在菩盧薩與普拉克里提的交互作用下而產生的;菩盧薩與普拉克里提的差別在於後者對前者是沒有任何影響的。此外,所有宇宙萬物皆自普拉克里提而來,所以普拉克里提是「眾因之因」(the cause of all causes),也就是「第一因」。事實上,也就是因為這樣的看法,原始版本的數論否認宇宙是由上帝創造的,認為「宇宙是由造物主創造」的說法是無法證實或證明的。[17]

從以上的說明可知,早期的數論認為宇宙萬物皆是由菩盧薩與普拉克里提組合而成的,其中菩盧薩是非物質的「神性我」,而普拉克里提則是具有各種變異性質的「物質我」;二者都是最終的「實相」(reality),而所有其他的元素皆自此演化而生,所以這個世界的本質是二元的。[18]

----

16 這裡的說明頗為粗略,因為不同的哲學派別對這二者都有不同的解釋。有興趣的讀者可參考 Chatterjee and Datta(2012)。

17 這裡其實有另一個重要的問題,那就是原始版本既然認為世界非上帝所造,因此也就不存在一位「人格化」(或稱「位格」)的上帝(或神)在背後主宰著宇宙萬物的演化。關於這個問題,《薄伽梵歌》第十二章中有深入的說明。

18 此處我們簡略地將「人」區分為「神性我」與「物質我」,不過這裡的物質其實只是指人事物中會變動的成分,所以也包含不具實體的能量。稍後我們會談到印度思想中的二元論與西方哲學的二元論是不同的。

　　換句話說，普拉克里提在早期的數論中，代表的是不包含「靈性」層面的原初物質，並沒有「造化」（Nature，大自然）的意思；造化是由菩盧薩與普拉克里提二者組成的。以人而言，每個人也都是由菩盧薩與普拉克里提二者組成，其中前者是我們永恆不變的神性我，而後者則是讓我們具備各種不同個性與特質的物質我。

　　但是何以創世之前的最終實相是菩盧薩與普拉克里提二者呢？如果普拉克里提是第一因，那麼菩盧薩又是自何而來？這兩者有因果關係嗎？如果普拉克里提是第一因，那麼必然就無其他任何東西可以獨立於普拉克里提之外。所以這樣的看法顯然是有問題的。如果我們再追根究底問下去，會發現最終的實相必然是「一」──所有一切皆自其而生。這個「一」就是老子所說的「道」，也是後來版本的數論對菩盧薩的「定義」。[19]

　　晚期印度教思想的發展（主要應該是受到《薄伽梵歌》的影響），把菩盧薩定義為最終的實相，是至上，是一切的一切，是上帝，所以也是絕對者（Absolute）；因為這無限的本質，所以有很多的名詞用來形容祂：梵（Brahman）、永恆聖靈、無上聖靈、上主、至上居所等等都是。[20]

　　在這較晚發展的看法中，認為普拉克里提是自菩盧薩而來，而宇宙種種再從普拉克里提中創生；普拉克里提被賦予的新定義是「造化」（在普羅希的英譯中，就是直接將普拉克里提譯為造化；因此以下我們就以造化來替代普拉克里提），我

---

19 《道德經》第廿五章：「有物混成，先天地生。寂兮寥兮，獨立不改，周行而不殆，可以為天下母。吾不知其名，字之曰道，強為之名曰大。」
20 梵（Brahman）一詞很容易與婆羅門（Brahmana, Brahmin）混淆，因為二者的英譯頗為接近。

們稍後再對造化做進一步闡述。

　　菩盧薩與造化的差別之一是，後者是被認知的對象（perceived），而前者是認知本體（perceiver）；一些學者稱前者為意識（consciousness），而後者為無意識（unconsciousness）。被認知者不可獨立於認知者之外，也就是無有菩盧薩即無造化，但菩盧薩卻可獨立於造化而存在，因此在這數論修正版本中，本質上是「一元論」的。[21] 克里希納在《薄伽梵歌》第七章第 12 節（以下以 7：12 表示）中說：

> 「不論他們生命的本質為何，是純真、熱情或是無明，他們都是從我而來。他們都是在我之中，但我卻不是在他們裡面。」

　　在另一句詩文中，克里希納說：

> 「……阿朱納啊！我只用我自己的小小一部分就維繫著這整個宇宙。」（10:42）

　　也就是菩盧薩包含造化，而不是造化包含菩盧薩。用數學的語言表達，就是造化包含於菩盧薩，是菩盧薩的子集合。因此上主——也就是菩盧薩——是超越一切造化的。

　　菩盧薩既「創」出造化，也進入萬物，成為萬物內在永恆的自性（Self），也就是阿特曼（ātman）、聖靈（Spirit）；這自性，

---

21 有些人將普拉克里提譯為「自性」，而將菩盧薩譯為「神我」，這比較符合早期數論的意涵，而與《薄伽梵歌》的看法並不一致。

以佛教的詞彙表達，就是佛性。我們的自性既自菩盧薩而來，可見我們的本質也是無限。但當我們為造化所惑，忘卻了我們的本來面目，我們就成為造化的一部分，成為有限的眾生。唯有當我們超越了造化的束縛，回憶起我們的本來面目與上主合一，才能再度成為無限。

造化與造化三性

前面提到造化來自菩盧薩，而造化的目的，根據數論，是將人束縛住。由於造化有生有滅，所以在某種意義上，造化是虛幻的，非最終之實相。克里希納說：

「不存在的（不真實的），永不成真；而存在的（真實的），也未曾有時成為虛妄；對於智者而言，這些真理不言自明。」（2:16）

祂所說的「不存在的（不真實的）」，就是造化；而「存在的（真實的）」，則是菩盧薩（無上聖靈）。[22] 造化在印度教與佛教經典中也稱為摩耶（Maya），其意即為幻象、幻影；老子《道德經》二十一章中也說：

「道之為物，惟恍惟惚。惚兮恍兮，其中有象；恍兮惚兮，其中有物。」

22《奇蹟課程》開宗明義也說：「凡是真實的，不受任何威脅，凡是不真實的，根本就不存在。上主的平安即在其中。」所表達的也是同樣的意義。

象與物，也就是造化，是「道」（菩盧薩）恍惚之間的一個幻夢。電影「駭客任務」（Matrix）中，由電腦虛擬的世界「母體」（Matrix），代表的就是造化，也就是我們所處的這個娑婆世界，其目的就是讓我們沉迷昏睡於其內。克里希納說：

「的確，這顯化於造化三性的神聖幻覺（摩耶）是難以超越的。只有完全奉獻於我，而且唯獨奉獻於我的人，才能做得到。」（7:14）

根據《梨俱吠陀》，造化係由三種性質（gunas、qualities、properties）或力量（forces）所組成，稱為造化三性（另譯「物質三性」或「三德」；第四道稱之為「三律」），分別是薩埵（Sattva）、羅闍（Rajas），與答磨（Tamas）。[23] 就好像作為我們基本遺傳因子的去氧核醣核酸（DNA）是由四種鹼基組合而成，而電腦的語言都是由 0 與 1 所組成的一樣，我們內在心理世界與外在的物質世界也完全是由造化三性組合而成；伊斯瓦蘭（1985）稱之為演化的力量（forces of evolution），頗為貼切。

歷來這三種性質的翻譯，不論中譯或英譯，都因不同譯者而有差異，也都各自捕捉了部分的梵文原意；有些譯本乾脆直接以梵文音譯呈現，而不作意譯。以下略述這三種性質（屬性）：

1.薩埵（悅性、喜、善）：包含了良善、純真、光明、和

---

23 將造化三性譯為三德頗有道家的意味，因為在老子《道德經》中，「道」與「德」原是不同的；譯者以為，道與德的關係猶如菩盧薩與造化的關係。《道德經》第三十八章中有言：「故失道而後德」，同樣，造化也是在離開菩盧薩的一體、無分別境界後而誕生的。

諧、平衡等性質。在造化中位於最高層。普羅希譯之為「純真」,「第四道」則稱之為「理智」,是不帶有情緒與昏睡的較高等性質。

2. 羅闍(變性、憂、激):代表可好可壞的能量,表現在人身上可稱之為熱情。透過個性,羅闍展現的內在是動機與野心,外在則是貪嗔恨。在造化中位於中間層。普羅希譯之為「熱情」(passion),葛吉夫稱之為「情感」,強調這個性質傾向於帶有情緒的面向。

3. 答磨(惰性、暗):包含了惰性(慣性)、懶惰、黑暗、無明(愚昧)、粗糙等性質。在造化中位於底層。普羅希譯之為「無明」,葛吉夫稱之為「機械」。第四道指出,機械式思維的思考是二元式的:非對即錯,非好即壞。凡事只要能「予以分類」或貼上標籤就算了事。這樣的思維停留在事物的極表層,甚或是以無明曲解事物,連表面的事實都看不到。

讓我們用一個心理學上的例子來說明造化三性的意涵。回顧近代西方心理學的發展,可發現近代心理學一直是以很唯物的方式在研究人類的心理,完全摒棄人的靈性層面;一些學派(如行為學派)甚至認為人的一切行為完全是制約下的結果。雖然也有一些心理學家(如美國心理學家威廉·詹姆士〔William James〕)探討靈性的議題,但多數仍是從機械式的物質觀點切入;似乎要到近年來舍利格曼(Martin E. P. Seligman)創立正向心理學(Positive Psychology),心理學界才開始正視靈性議題(如靜坐)的重要性。[24]

----

24 如心理學功能學派創始人威廉·詹姆士就著有《宗教經驗之種種》,從心理層面探討超

舍利格曼觀察到過去幾十年心理分析、心理治療等雖大行其道，但憂鬱症、躁鬱症等心理疾病卻更加肆虐，因而開始思考心理學到底出了什麼問題，而人又應如何自處才能獲得幸福快樂。如今正向心理學已有一些研究成果與成效，也肯定了靈性與靜坐冥思角色的重要；由於學者與研究者們在學校與社區的大力推廣，近年來正向心理學的理念越來越受到大眾的注意與重視。

回顧正向心理學的發展過程，可發現與舍利格曼在 1960 年代發現的「習得的無助」（learned helplessness）有很大的關連。[25] 舍利格曼在當研究生時，曾經參與一個研究團隊，利用巴甫洛夫（Pavlov）的古典制約理論，以動物實驗研究個體在面對恐懼時，如何調適其行為。[26] 作法是將一隻狗放在一個實驗箱的地板上，地板是可通電流的。他們原先的想法是：將電擊與一信號配對，當狗遭到電擊並聽到信號後，會跳離原地；一旦制約完成，狗只要聽到信號聲，就會產生恐懼並跳離原處，即使實際上並沒有電擊。

實驗結果顯示，一般而言，狗在受到電擊後，的確如預期地會馬上離開原有位置——這其實就是動性、變性——我們受

感官經驗。有趣的是，詹姆士去世之後，竟然透過近代著名靈媒珍・羅伯茲（Jane Roberts），寫了一本書，書名為《一位美國哲學家的死後日記：威廉・詹姆士的世界觀》，於其中大談潛意識與靈性等諸多議題。

25 以下這個例子取自舍利格曼（1998）的《學習樂觀、樂觀學習》一書。

26 從靈性的角度來看，所有加諸眾生的痛苦都是有違愛心與非暴力的最基本原則的，因此對動物會造成身心傷害的動物實驗是不可取的。譯者採用這個例子的原意，僅在說明近代心理學研究已提供科學證據，支持古老靈性經典的觀點；這對一些現代科學的擁護者在瞭解經典上，似乎是有幫助的。儘管如此，譯者仍在此致上衷心的歉意，也希望未來的科學實驗能在符合靈性原則的前提下進行。

到外在負面刺激的立即反應一向是：馬上行動以避開衝擊；這種反應可說是我們最原始的反應，但卻不是理性或理智的反應。通常而言，這種反應或行動也都伴隨著騷動的情緒。

令研究人員驚訝的是，有些狗完全不逃避電擊，動也不動，只是消極地坐在通電的地板上哀鳴。這讓研究人員相當無奈，實驗只好中斷、放棄。但舍利格曼發現，這些狗其實是在先前的實驗過程中學得了「無助」，所以才選擇放棄：因為怎麼做都逃脫不了被電擊的命運，那麼又何必採取行動呢？這正是惰性支配下的結果，也就是內心的無明與恐懼大到壓抑了所有行動的驅力；由此可見，相對於變性而言，惰性是更深的黑暗。

惰性的反應機制是不面對──通常採取的「作法」是忽略、忽視，甚至以酒精、毒品、巫術等來麻痺自己內心的感受。以人類行為而言，舍利格曼發現一些人在面對困境與挫折時，連試都不試就放棄；他認為這種面對困境時所產生的無助感（他稱之為「習得的無助」），與幼年時期的成長經驗有很大的關係。

假如狗能從實驗中觀察到每當研究人員出現，或聽到研究人員坐下來的聲音（又或許是聽到電源啟動的聲音），接下來很快就會有電擊的話，牠就可以有所提防，像是先行離開原處；或至少心理有所準備，也就不會這麼受到驚嚇──這就是「悅性」、「智性」的呈現。可見悅性少了另兩種性質所伴隨的騷動、痛苦的情緒，而多了一分平靜與平和。但這樣的智性展現，似乎只有較高等的動物才比較明顯。

可以想像當我們與上主（道）「分離」，剎那間體驗到有限的「我」（I-ness, self）時，是多麼地恐懼而驚慌失措；而變性、惰性與悅性正是依序反應而發展出來的三種力量。正因如此，第四道稱此「三律」為正向力（積極力、主動力）、反向力（消極力、被動力）與中和力。根據數論，這三種性質是構成造化的基本元素，所有造化中的每一事物都含有這三性，只是組合各有不同。[27]《薄伽梵歌》指出，三性的不同，不但呈現在人的個性、信仰上，甚至也反映在食物上。

雖然從表面上看起來，薩埵是悅性、純真、良善，所以應該是「較好」的，但《薄伽梵歌》也提醒我們，這三者的目的都是將我們束縛在造化之內。

無罪的人啊！三者中，純真是潔亮、強壯而不受傷害的，但因著其對幸福與開悟的渴求而把人束縛住。

熱情，由對享樂與執著的欲望所驅使，因著其對行動的喜愛而把靈魂束縛住。

無明（愚昧）——黑暗的產物，以環環相連的愚行、懶惰與昏睡，來蒙蔽眾生的感官。（14:6–14:8）

的確，只要有「我」，認為我是這個作為者，就是在造化之內。克里希納在《薄伽梵歌》中一再地提醒我們，唯有獻祭一切作為，作為供養，無我地奉獻上主，否則都難以獲得終究

---

27 道德經第四十二章所揭示的「道生一，一生二，二生三，三生萬物」，也頗有造化三性的意味。

的自在解脫。儘管如此，悅性、純真也的確是「較好」的，因為透過它我們得以通往智慧，也減少了修行上的障礙。可見真正的問題核心並不是我們的身口意是否符合悅性，而是我們心中對於悅性的執著。

由於本中譯版是以普羅希的英譯為本，所以我們在正文中依普羅希的翻譯，將此三性譯為「純真」、「熱情」與「無明」（愚昧）；但這樣的翻譯是有些失真的，因此有必要再一次提醒讀者。以羅闍為例，普羅希將之譯為 "passion"，中文可直譯為熱情或激情；但不論是熱情或激情，都未能完全反映出羅闍這個詞中所隱含的騷動情緒或情感的意味。

造化廿四締

數論認為，在造化三性的互動下，宇宙萬物應運而生。此一演化過程可以總結為「造化廿四締」（請見下頁圖），也就是造化的廿四原則（tattvas）。造化是第一締，也就是第一個自菩盧薩創出的。[28] 當造化三性三種力量處於均衡的狀態，造化也呈現「未顯」的型態；造化與菩盧薩的互動下，造成造化三性三種力量的消長，進一步促成造化的「顯化」，依序創出菩提智、我執與心；而感官與五大元素則由心幻化而生。根據數論，菩提智、我執與心等基本上都是無意識的，唯有透過菩盧薩的「光」，思想、心智活動等才可能覺醒。

造化之各原則簡述如下：

1. 菩提智（Buddhi，一譯「覺」；Mahat）：普羅希譯之為

---

28 另一種說法是把菩盧薩納入，統稱為「數論廿五締」。

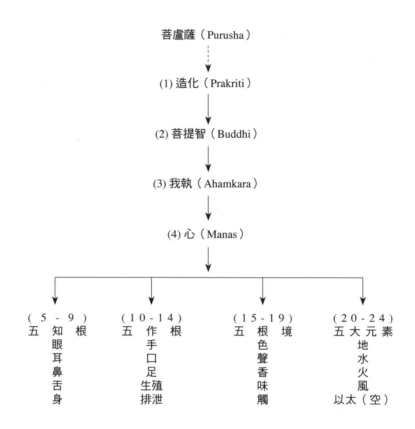

理智或理性。雖名為菩提智，但並非真正的智慧，只是思維的能力；它仍是造化的產物，受到造化三性的影響。菩提智也稱「大一」（the great one），因為接下來的「我執」與「心」皆是自其演化而來，但也有人認為「大一」指的是造化，而不是菩提智。

2. 我執（ego-sense; Ahamkara）：也有人譯為「我慢」，但其實是「自我感」，也就是分離或隔離的感覺：感覺到自我與

他人、眾生的不同，以及與外界隔離的感覺；相當於佛教唯識論所說的第七識，也就是末那識。普羅希譯之為「個性」，是很貼切的。我們因為認同了「我」（小我），而經驗到有限。[29]在《薄伽梵歌》中，阿朱納就是這自我的象徵，更可說是造化的「核心」。我們輪迴受苦雖是因這我執，但了悟解脫也需靠這我執。

3. 心（mind; Manas）：也稱「意根」，與「五知根」合稱「六根」。心被認為是感官的控制者，五知根與五作根是在心的指令下而運作的。[30] 從「造化廿四締」可看出，心位於我執（自我）與十根之間，扮演協調的角色。克里希納說：

「他當藉其最高的心靈之協助以求得解脫，且不貶抑他自己的心靈。因為心靈雖是他唯一的朋友；但也可成為他的敵人。」（6:5）

4. 五知根（five organs of perception; five sense organs）：五種認知的器官（感官），即眼、耳、鼻、舌、身。

5. 五作根（five organs of action）：與行動、行為有關的五種器官，即手、口、足、生殖與排泄。

6. 五根境（five subtle elements）：五種細微元素，即色、聲、香、味、觸，也稱「五塵」。

----

29 就像是《聖經》創世記中，亞當與夏娃吃了知識之樹的果實，眼睛亮了起來，才開始有了自我的個別身分，時間也自此展開；在此之前，他們是與上帝合一的，當然也就沒有時間這種概念的存在。

30 數論中的心（Manas），其梵文與佛教唯識論的第七識「末那」同，但意義上有所不同。

7. 五大元素（five gross elements）：五種粗略元素，即地、水、火、風、以太（空）。

數論認為在造化造出菩提智、我執與心後，當薩埵成為主導力量下，才進一步造出五知根。當羅闍力量主導又從五知根中演化出五作根；而當答磨力量主導時，才演化出五種細微元素與五種粗略元素。五知根與五作根合稱「十根」，是屬於外在器官；心與我執、菩提智三者則稱為內在器官。這些外在器官與內在器官加起來，又合稱「十三根」。

數論與佛教同樣有「一切唯心造」的看法。從「造化廿四締」圖可看出，身（由 5-19 締構成）與身外之宇宙（由 20-24 締組成）皆由心所造；至於心之後的主導者，則是「我」的幻覺（我慢）。宇宙演化的歷史就是造化廿四締作用的結果。《薄伽梵歌》中，對廿四締的論述頗多，因為造化的力量的確不可思議。克里希納說：

「人們說感官的力量強大，但感官之後還有心，心之後則是理智，而比理智更偉大的則是祂──上主。」（3:42）

修行解脫的確需對感官、心、理智下功夫，但更重要的，是專注於比造化更高的上主。

四種瑜伽與第四道

「瑜伽」（yoga）的原意就是「合一」（union），也就是與上主合一之道。在《薄伽梵歌》中，克里希納談論到四種瑜伽，

也就是四條修行的道路：

1. 羯磨瑜伽（Karma yoga）：行動之道，更明確的說，是無我行動之道；修行者透過全心無我的服務眾生，而自有限的自我中解脫。

2. 闍那瑜伽（Jnana yoga）：知識或智慧之道；修行者透過意志與明辨能力，將自我從對身、心與感官的認同中解放出來。

3. 巴克提瑜伽（Bhakti yoga）：奉愛之道；修行者透過完全奉獻（獻身）於上主的愛中而臻於無上。

4. 禪那瑜伽（Dhyana yoga）：禪定之道；修行者透過靜坐冥思，降伏意念與感官，從而自性於定中顯現。[31] 印度教的傳承中，禪定瑜伽尤其是指勝王（Raja）瑜伽。[32]

由於造化使然，我們每個人了悟自性、回歸上帝的方式也不盡相同。在這方面，譯者認為第四道有些不錯的觀點，在此作一點補充。

第四道認為人的「機能」可以分成七個中心，包括四個低等中心（本能中心、運動中心、情感中心、理智中心）、性中心，以及兩個高等中心（高等情感中心與高等理智中心）。[33] 所謂的「修行」是發展兩個高等中心，但要能完備地發展高等中心，有賴於四個低等中心的平衡發展。這是因為多數一般人在

---

31 在中文裡，常有將闍那與禪定混為一談的。追根究底，大概是因為禪定的巴利文是jhana（早期經典譯為「禪那」，也意譯為「止觀」，後來簡稱為禪），而闍那的梵文為jnana；二者只差一個字母，而 h 與 n 這兩個字母的外型又很接近。

32 張澄基《佛學今詮》第五章〈禪那瑜伽〉中，對勝王瑜伽的修行次第有頗為詳盡的解說。

33 這兩個高等中心有點像是佛教所說的「悲」與「智」，不過這裡的慈悲與智慧是更深一層的「同體大悲」與「無分別智」。

先天上都會有過度認同某些中心的傾向，因而阻礙了高等中心的發展。由於在這些低等中心上的不同傾向，第四道認為一般人可分成三種人：

1. 第一種人的重心傾向於本能中心與運動中心。在修行上，這樣的人也傾向於從身體與行動上去下功夫，尤其是修身體上的苦行，這樣的道路歸類為「第一道」。

2. 第二種人的重心傾向於情感中心。在修行上，這樣的人傾向於從情感與信心去著手，這樣的道路歸類為「第二道」。

3. 第三種人的重心傾向於理智中心。在修行上，這樣的人也傾向於從知識去著手，這樣的道路歸類為「第三道」。

由此可見第一種人傾向於行動之道，第二種人傾向於奉愛之道，而第三種人則傾向於知識之道。鄔斯賓斯基在《第四道》中評述：這些道路在許多方面都很有效力，但也都容易流於過度而沒有彈性。

因為我們既然身處造化，就必受造化三性的影響。我們以情感中心的人（第二種人）為例，簡單說明造化三性對宗教信仰的影響。如果是變性（熱情）主導，傾向於情感中心的人只想著宗教可為自己帶來的好處。內心只是想著獨善其身，即使是布施，也只是想著可以為自己的未來帶來什麼福報。

如果是惰性（無明）主導，重心在感情中心的人可能會執著於盲目的信仰，變成宗教狂，也可能以宗教之名行權力追求之實，以滿足自己的私欲。殊不見各種修行團體中，雖都是志同道合的「同修」，但追求名利、權力的爭鬥卻仍如家常便飯；宗教的本質至此更是喪失殆盡，徒具形式與外表。更有甚者，

是心中為負面、黑暗的情緒所淹沒，因而服從於邪惡的力量，以暴力對待他人。甚至可能發動「聖戰」去毀滅其他所謂的「異教徒」，心中深信是「上帝的旨意」。這些宗教暴力事件在人類的歷史中屢見不鮮，可說完全與宗教所提倡的愛的本質背離。

如果是悅性（純真）主導的話，重心在感情中心的人會從內在去走修行的道路，甚至也會因著對上主與眾生的愛而化為外在的行動。這樣的人顯然在三者間，最貼近靈性的本質。只是如果仍執著於「我」，不論這樣的我有多細微，終究仍會把人束縛在造化之內。

可見各條修行道路並無優劣之分，而是人的特質、程度，各有不同。同樣地，宗教也沒有高低之別，而是信眾、信徒的內在因造化三性主導力量的不同而有差異。因此，當我們真正的瞭解，會發現只有一種宗教，也就是帶領我們了悟自性、回歸上帝的宗教；但當我們為我執所惑，會發現每個人都自有一個宗教，儘管宗教的名稱是一樣的。

「第四道」所主張的，就是不偏於任何一條道路：重要的不是放棄外在的事物，而是從內在去下功夫。這其實正是克里希納在《薄伽梵歌》中所表達的觀點。例如，克里希納雖特別讚揚了禪定瑜伽：

「智者（瑜伽修行者）勝於苦行者，也勝於學者與行動者，因此阿朱納啊！當一位智者（瑜伽修行者）吧。」（6:46）

但事實上，《薄伽梵歌》認為每一條道路都是必要的，其實也都是同樣的一條路。我們看到不同的道路，是因為有分別心。例如，在談到智慧之道時，克里希納也談到靜坐與捨棄行為的價值（4:41）。而靜坐顯然也需智慧的輔助，以收攝感官與欲望（6:24-25）。在談到行動之道時，克里希納雖也說正行（正確行為）之道較捨棄行為佳（5:2），但也說不開悟的人才會把智慧與正行看成兩回事（5:4）。

不論是哪一條瑜伽之道，《薄伽梵歌》中都強調捨棄（renunciation；也譯「出離」）；一般人以為捨棄是指放下外在的一切，但克里希納強調真正的放下、捨棄，是內在的不執著。克里希納說：

「知識優於盲目的行動，靜坐冥想優於僅僅擁有知識，而對於行為果實之捨棄則又優於靜坐冥想。只要有捨棄，就有平安。」（12:12）

一點啟示

《奧義書》中，以駕馭馬車來比喻人：馬車象徵肉身，理智是馬夫，紛飛散漫的意念是韁繩，感官是馬，馳騁於欲望的道路上。我們的自性是主人，但卻任由馬車四處奔散。

我們在這個娑婆世界「玩」久了，不免誤以為自己就是這馬車。這就是佛家所說的「我執」（ego），也就是「小我」（self）。佛家所說的執著（attachment），第四道稱之為「認

同」（identification）。榮格的分析心理學認為，我們所認同的，形成了我們的個性（personality），而不認同的，則被打入意識的冷宮，成為「陰影」（shadow）（其實也還是認同）。這些都是潛意識（無意識）的內容。

在《薄伽梵歌》中，般度五子代表的是我們認同的個性，而持國百子正是我們不認同的陰影。不論認同與否，都是小我的一部分。小我既是造化所為，所以也是虛妄而不永恆的。克里希納在《薄伽梵歌》中一再地提醒我們，應平等看待一切二元對立的事物：好惡、成敗、榮辱、冷熱等皆然；從內在捨棄，不執著，並時時專注於至上。在《薄伽梵歌》中，克里希納不親身參與戰爭，卻擔任阿朱納的馬夫，正意味著我們應讓上主成為我們的馭者（就像基督宗教常用的一句話：「耶和華是我的牧者」，二者可說同義）。

總結來說，《薄伽梵歌》有兩個主要啟示：第一是捨棄與臣服。捨棄是放下對外在事物、內在欲望與感官感受的執著；臣服則是更進一步放下自我，將自己交給上主，全然地接受上主為我們所作的任何安排。臣服並不是印度教的特有觀點，基督宗教與伊斯蘭教（尤其是其密教中的蘇非教派）也有同樣看法。[34] 在《薄伽梵歌》的最後一章中，克里希納說：

> 「所有的作為都依靠我，而且都是為我而作，藉著我的恩典，他證得了永恆不變之生命。」

----

34 佛教雖沒有臣服於上主的觀點（因為佛教被認為是「無神論」），但在其密教裡，也同樣有臣服於上師的想法。

「因此在行動作為上臣服於我，安住於我之內，將理智專
注於我，而且心中總是想著我。」

「心念完全繫於我，如此因著我的恩典你將克服你道途上
的障礙。」（18:56-58）

所有的修行道路到此匯成了一條道路：這是奉愛之道，也
是行動之道，同時也是知識與禪定之道；唯有在行動作為、頭
腦（心念與理智）、情感，所有一切都臣服於至上，我們才能
與上主合一。

《薄伽梵歌》的第二個啟示，或許也是最重要的啟示，是
克里希納在這場對話的終尾對阿朱納所說的：

「……你是我所摯愛的。」（18:64–18:65）

這其實也是上主對我們的保證──仿如是祂在我們耳邊不
斷地輕聲提醒──因為我們原本就是上帝的子女。我們在世間
汲汲營營、為名為利，無非也都只是反映著我們內心對愛的需
要與渴望而已。耶穌不也說：

「所以我告訴你們，不要為生命憂慮吃什麼，為身體憂慮
穿什麼；因為生命勝於飲食，身體勝於衣裳。你想烏鴉，也不
種也不收，又沒有倉又沒有庫，神尚且養活牠。你們比飛鳥是
何等的貴重呢！你們哪一個能用思慮使壽數多加一刻呢？這
最小的事，你們尚且不能作，為什麼還憂慮其餘的事呢？你

想百合花怎麼長起來；它也不勞苦，也不紡線。然而我告訴你們，就是所羅門極榮華的時候，他所穿戴的，還不如這花一朵呢！你們這小信的人哪，野地裡的草今天還在，明天就丟在爐裡，神還給它這樣的妝飾，何況你們呢！你們不要求吃什麼，喝什麼，也不要罣心；這都是外邦人所求的。你們必須用這些東西，你們的父是知道的。你們只要求他的國，這些東西就必加給你們了。你們這小群，不要懼怕，因為你們的父樂意把國賜給你們。你們要變賣所有的賙濟人，為自己預備永不壞的錢囊，用不盡的財寶在天上，就是賊不能近、蟲不能蛀的地方。因為，你們的財寶在那裡，你們的心也在那裡。」（路加福音12:22-34）

只要捨棄與臣服，並專注於上主，我們終可感受到上主無所不在的愛，就永不匱乏。

（這章雖說是導讀，但闡釋的僅僅是譯者個人的觀點，而不是《薄伽梵歌》的直接教導，因此也可能只對某些讀者在研讀《薄伽梵歌》之初有些助益，但卻不是所有讀者都需要的。）

- Chapter -

1

....

阿朱納的消沉意志
The Despondency of Arjuna

本章為這場對話揭開序幕。一開始是由持國王的大臣山佳亞透過靈視,將對峙於戰場上的雙方陣容與戰情,敘述給持國王聽。

在雙方蓄勢待發時刻,阿朱納王子請擔任馭者的克里希納,將馬車駛至雙方陣營之間,讓他觀察戰場局勢。當阿朱納看到彼此為敵的雙方陣營裡,都是自己的親戚朋友時,突然感到灰心喪志,不禁質疑起這場戰爭的意義究竟為何。由此進而引出克里希納道出許多有關生命的意義與宇宙本質的奧秘。

歷來許多譯注者都稱這個俱盧戰場為「法性戰場」(dharmakshetra),代表我們的肉身;持國王代表我們盲目的心靈(也就是數論中所說的我執),為感官(十根)所左右(持國百子即代表這十根的各種作用);般度五子則代表我們七個脈輪中較低的五個脈輪。印度瑜伽認為人的中脈(大約是脊椎)共有七個脈輪(chakras,能量中心),由下至上分別是海底輪、臍輪、太陽神經叢(太陽輪)、心輪、喉輪、眉心輪與頂輪。而了悟、開悟,或與上帝合一的過程,就是克服我執、感官,將意識由低等能量中心提升到高等能量中心的奮鬥過程;在此,克里希納代表頂輪。

如果把這場戰爭看成是內在戰爭,那麼以榮格分析心理學的術語來說,這個戰場就是我們的潛意識(unconsciousness,或譯「無意識」),阿朱納是自我(self、ego),居於核心位置;般度諸子陣營代表的是我們認同的部分,形成我們的個性;而持國諸子則是代表我們不接受的部分,形成我們的陰影。

更深一點探析,可發現持國諸子一方雖代表敵營,但是

其中卻有許多我們的親友。這意味著我們雖然不喜歡這些「陰影」，但這些內在不接受的陰影卻是陪伴著我們成長至今，有些甚至與我們很親密（或曾經很親密）。從心理學的角度來看，這些陰影並不是全然無價值的：它們有些是個體在成長過程（尤其是幼年時期）為了存活而發展出來的反應機制（防衛機轉）。只是這些制約機制一旦形成，就變成「我」的一部分，在日後經歷類似或相呼應的情境時，自行啟動運作。

我們一生都為潛意識所主導，在認同與不認同間擺盪掙扎（用第四道的用語來說，我們是在昏睡，不是真正的清醒，而生命的意義正是追求覺醒）。但不論是個性或陰影，都是執著、我執，都是「我」的一部分；唯有接受這一切，生命才會圓滿──「接受」是了悟到不論是我們認同或不認同的，這一切種種都是造化所為；來自無限至上的自性（Self、ātman），才是我們真正的本來面目。

在《奧義書》中，馬車象徵肉身，理智是馬夫，紛飛散漫的意念是韁繩，感官是馬，馳騁於欲望的道路上；自性是主人，卻任由馬車四處奔散。在《薄伽梵歌》中，克里希納不親身參與戰爭，卻擔任阿朱納的馬夫，正意味著我們應讓上主成為我們的馭者；戰場上的一切都是造化所為，但上主卻是超越理智、超越一切的。

1. 持國王問道：山佳亞啊！此刻在我方與般度諸子對峙的俱盧神聖戰場上，情況如何呢？

2. 山佳亞答道：面對般度軍隊的陣列，難敵王子走到他的古魯德羅那跟前，言道：[1]

3. 「師尊！請看這般度諸子的強大軍隊，此刻正列陣於您聰慧的徒弟——木柱王之子（猛光）的面前。[2]

4. 「其中盡是英雄與偉大的射手：在戰鬥上，足以與阿朱納、怖軍匹比的尤猶旦納、毗羅達，以及木柱王；他們全都是偉大的戰士。

5. 「勇旗、顯光、英勇的迦尸王、普盧吉、昆提伯亞、賽夫亞，都是人中之選；[3]

6. 「尤達曼奴、烏塔摩加、首哈德拉，與德羅帕蒂（黑公主）的兒子們；他們都是名人。[4]

7. 「再來，請看看我方的將領們。最好的靈性導師啊！我方軍隊的領袖，我將為您一一道來。

---

1 這裡的古魯（guru）係指老師，但更是指靈性的導師、上師。這裡譯者採用音譯，這樣較能保留多一點這個詞的靈性意味。

2 德羅那原是雙方陣營許多將士的老師，但在此戰中，他隸屬於持國王諸子陣營。

3 這裡的迦尸（Kashi）是古稱，於 1985 年改名為瓦拉那西（Varanasi），另一舊名為波羅奈（Banares，也譯「貝拿勒斯」）。該城位於北方邦的東南部，坐落於恆河之濱，是印度教七大聖地之一。佛陀初轉法輪的鹿野苑（Sarnath）就在該城北方十公里。

4 德羅帕蒂（黑公主）為般度五子的共同妻子，她為般度五子每人生了一個兒子。

The King Dhritarashtra asked:

1. O Sanjaya! What happened on the sacred battlefield of Kurukshetra,when my people gathered against the Pandavas?

Sanjaya replied:

2. The Prince Duryodhana, when he saw the army of the Pandavas paraded, approached his preceptor Guru Drona and spoke as follows:

3. "Revered Father! Behold this mighty host of the Pandavas, paraded by the son of King Drupada, your wise disciple.

4. "In it are heroes and great bowmen; the equals in battle of Arjuna and Bhima, Yuyudhana, Virata and Drupada, great soldiers all;

5. "Dhrishtaketu, Chekitan, the valiant King of Benares, Purujit, Kuntibhoja, Shaivya – a master over many;

6. "Yudhamanyu, Uttamauja, Saubhadra and the sons of Draupadi, famous men.

7. "Further, take note of all those captains who have ranged themselves on our side, O best of spiritual guides! the leaders of my army. I will name them for you.

8.「首先是您；再來是偉大的戰士：毗濕摩、卡爾納、克里帕；還有馬勇、維卡納與日授王之子（廣聲）；[5]

9.「還有許多許多，他們都準備好要為我而死；他們全副武裝，且都精於戰鬥。

10.「儘管有毗濕摩為主帥，但我軍似乎較弱；敵軍雖以怖軍為主帥，卻似乎是較強的。[6]

11.「所有軍士皆依戰鬥位置列隊堅守崗位；所有的將軍全都守護於主帥毗濕摩周圍。」[7]

12. 接著，為鼓舞士氣，英勇的祖父毗濕摩，這位俱盧族的最年長者，吹響他的海螺，聲如獅吼。[8]

13. 緊接著所有的海螺、戰鼓、喇叭與號角齊響，聲音響徹雲霄。

14. 接著，坐在套著白馬的大戰車中的克里希納與阿朱納，也吹起了他們的神聖號角。

5　卡爾納為阿朱納之母昆蒂在嫁給般度王之前所生之子。但此一秘密除了昆蒂外，沒有人知道。在此戰役中，卡爾納身處持國百子陣營，反而與自己的兄弟為敵。

6　有些譯者對這句詩文感到有些困惑，因為事實上持國子嗣的軍隊在數量與陣容上，都是比較強大的，似乎不太應該由難敵王子口中說出這樣的話。因此有些譯本在翻譯時，把詩文中兩軍的強弱對調。前面曾提到這場大戰象徵我們內在的征戰。代表內在陰影的難敵陣營，其實在內心深處知道小我是不可能戰勝上主的。從這個觀點來看，或許難敵的確是因為般度的軍隊有克里希納在，而覺得對方較強。這裡，譯者採用原文。

7　按照文義，3-11 這九句詩文是難敵王子所言；從下一句起，又回到山佳亞對戰場的敘述。

8　毗濕摩是持國與般度的伯父，所以是持國百子與般度五子的伯祖父。

8. "You come first; then Bhishma, Karna, Kripa, great soldiers; Ashvatthama, Vikarna and the son of Somadatta;

9. "And many others, all ready to die for my sake; all armed, all skilled in war.

10. "Yet our army seems the weaker, though commanded by Bhishma; their army seems the stronger, though commanded by Bhima.

11. "Therefore in the rank and file, let all stand firm in their posts, according to battalions; and all you generals about Bhishma."

12. Then to enliven his spirits, the brave Grandfather Bhishma, eldest of the Kuru-clan, blew his conch till it sounded like a lion's roar.

13. And immediately all the conches and drums, the trumpets and horns, blared forth in tumultuous uproar.

14. Then seated in their spacious war chariot, yoked with white horses, Lord Shri Krishna and Arjuna sounded their divine shells.

15. 克里希納吹起他的潘查衍那螺、阿朱納吹起他的德瓦達塔螺，勇猛的怖軍也吹起他知名的龐德拉螺。

16. 昆蒂之子堅陣王吹響他的阿難它維加雅、無種與偕天則分別吹起夙苟薩與牟尼菩虛帕卡。

17. 還有偉大的射手迦尸王、勇士希坎狄，與所向無敵的猛光、維拉塔與善戰的薩特亞奇。

18. 王啊！木柱王、德羅帕蒂之子們與勇士首哈德拉也吹起他們的海螺。

19. 喧囂之聲撼動持國王子嗣之心，回聲驚天動地。

20. 接著，在繪有猴神哈奴曼的旗幟下，阿朱納看著戰場上準備迎戰的持國百子們。

21. 阿朱納舉起了他的弓，對克里希納說：「永無過失者啊！世尊！請將馬車駕至兩軍之間，

22.「讓我可以看到是誰與我並肩而戰，是誰對我開戰；

23.「也讓我瞧瞧這些急於取悅那罪孽深重的持國王之子的軍士們。」

24. 山佳亞道：聽到阿朱納的請求，克里希納將祂閃亮的馬車駕至兩方軍隊的正中間，

15. Lord Shri Krishna blew His Panchajanya and Arjuna his Devadatta, brave Bhima his renowned shell, Paundra.

16. The King Dharmaraja, the son of Kunti, blew the Anantavijaya, Nakula and Sahadeva, the Sughosha and Manipushpaka, respectively.

17. And the Maharaja of Benares, the great archer; Shikhandi, the great soldier; Dhrishtadyumna, Virata and Satyaki, the invincible.

18. And O King! Drupada, the sons of Draupadi and Saubhadra, the great soldier, blew their conches.

19. The tumult rent the hearts of the sons of Dhritarashtra, and violently shook heaven and earth with its echo.

20. Then beholding the sons of Dhritarashtra, drawn up on the battlefield, ready to begin the fight, Arjuna, whose flag bore the Hanuman.

21. Raising his bow, spoke thus to the Lord Shri Krishna: "O Infallible! Lord of the earth! Please draw up my chariot between the two armies.

22. "So that I may observe those who must fight on my side, those who must fight against me;

23. "And gaze over this array of soldiers, eager to please the sinful son of Dhritarashtra."

Sanjaya said:

24. Having listened to the request of Arjuna, Lord Shri Krishna drew up His bright chariot exactly in the midst between the two armies,

25. 就在這些由毗濕摩與德羅那領軍的邦主之前，克里希納說道：「阿朱納啊！看看聚集於此的俱盧族成員們。」

26. 阿朱納注意到有眾父輩、祖輩、叔伯、表親、子、孫、師、友，

27. 以及岳父與盟友，分布於雙方陣營之中。阿朱納注視著眼前的親族，

28. 滿懷憐憫之心，悲戚言道：「啊！我的主啊！當我看著所有這些渴望戰鬥的同胞，

29. 「我的四肢不聽使喚、口乾舌燥、渾身顫抖，且汗毛直豎。

30. 「我的甘迪瓦弓從手中滑落，全身肌膚灼熱。我無法保持冷靜，因我心亂如麻。

31. 「我有不祥之兆；於戰場之上戮殺自己的人民，何祥之有？

32. 「喔！主啊！我既不渴望勝利，也不渴求王國與快樂。王國、幸福與生命，對我有何意義，

33. 「如果這些東西的代價是他們的財產與生命？因為我之所以追求這些，正是為了他們：

34. 「師輩、父輩、祖輩、子孫、叔伯、岳父、同襟，與其他親人。

25. Whither Bhishma and Drona had led all the rulers of the earth, and spoke thus: O Arjuna! Behold these members of the family of Kuru assembled.

26. There Arjuna noticed fathers, grandfathers, uncles, cousins, sons, grandsons, teachers, friends;

27. Fathers-in-law and benefactors, arrayed on both sides. Arjuna then gazed at all those kinsmen before him.

28. And his heart melted with pity and sadly he spoke: "O my Lord! When I see all these, my own people, thirsting for battle.

29. "My limbs fail me and my throat is parched, my body trembles and my hair stands on end.

30. "The bow Gandiva slips from my hand, and my skin burns. I cannot keep quiet, for my mind is in tumult.

31. "The omens are adverse; what good can come from the slaughter of my people on this battlefield?

32. "Ah my Lord! I crave not for victory, nor for the kingdom, nor for any pleasure. What were a kingdom or happiness or life to me.

33. "When those for whose sake I desire these things stand here about to sacrifice their property and their lives:

34. "Teachers, fathers and grandfathers, sons and grandsons, uncles, father-in-law, brothers-in-law and other relatives.

35.「即使為擁有三界，我也不願殺他們，更何況是為此寂寥大地？這更甚於戮及吾身。[9]

36.「我的主啊！持國王子嗣們的死亡能帶來什麼快樂呢？殺了這些險惡之徒，只是徒增罪孽罷了。

37.「與其屠殺親人，也就是這些持國王的子嗣們，我們更應有高雅的功業，因為，主啊，我們怎能由殺害親族而得到幸福呢？

38.「雖然這些為貪婪所蒙蔽的人，並不認為毀損親族或與友為敵有何罪業，

39.「然則雙目清明的我們，既然瞭解摧毀家園之錯謬，難道不應避開以免犯此大罪嗎？

40.「家族之毀同時也意味著古老傳承之毀，而當這些都失落了，不道德（不信宗教）將遍及家園。

41.「一旦道德淪喪，家中婦女的行為將會開始背離；當她們失去了純潔，種姓混亂也就應運而生。

42.「種姓混亂毀了家族，而犯下這些罪行的人，也毀了自己。祖先無人祭祀，祖靈也將瀕危。

9　這裡「三界」泛指天上、人間與地下三世界；佛教思想中，三界是欲界、色界與無色界，其中各自又有各種不同的世界。不論這裡的三界所指為何，基本上，三界都是屬於成住壞空的非永恆世界。

35. "I would not kill them, even for three worlds; why then for this poor earth? It matters not if I myself am killed.

36. "My Lord! What happiness can come from the death of these sons of Dhritarashtra? We shall sin if we kill these desperate men.

37. "We are worthy of a nobler feat than to slaughter our relatives -the sons of Dhritarashtra; for, my Lord! how can we be happy if we kill our kinsmen?

38. "Although these men, blinded by greed, see no guilt in destroying their kin or fighting against their friends,

39. "Should not we, whose eyes are open, who consider it to be wrong to annihilate our house, turn away from so great a crime?

40. "The destruction of our kindred means the destruction of the traditions of our ancient lineage, and when these are lost, irreligion will overrun our homes.

41. "When irreligion spreads, the women of the house begin to stray; when they lose their purity, adulteration of the stock follows.

42. "Promiscuity ruins both the family and those who defile it; while the souls of our ancestors droop, through lack of the funeral cakes and ablutions.

43.「摧毀傳承、玷污血脈,古老種姓的傳統與家族的純正也將淪喪。

44.「主啊!智者說:失去古老傳統者將永遠失落。

45.「唉!為了享有王國之樂,竟然願意去殺害同胞、犯下重罪,豈不怪哉!

46.「與其如此,還不如讓持國王之子,以他們手中的武器殺死手無寸鐵、毫不抵抗的我,這肯定對我還好一些!」

47. 山佳亞道:阿朱納說完了這些話,就在這大軍之中,頹坐於座中,拋開他的弓與箭,哀慟不已。

這就是聖靈的科學與自我認識的藝術、奧義書之一的聖典——《薄伽梵歌》中,克里希納與阿朱納王子對話的第一章,名為「阿朱納的消沉意志」。

43. "By the destruction of our lineage and the pollution of blood, ancient class traditions and family purity alike perish.

44. "The wise say, my Lord! that they are forever lost, whose ancient traditions are lost.

45. "Alas, it is strange that we should be willing to kill our own countrymen and commit a great sin, in order to enjoy the pleasures of a kingdom.

46. "If, on the contrary, the sons of Dhritarashtra, with weapons in their hands, should slay me, unarmed and unresisting, surely that would be better for my welfare!"

Sanjaya said:

47. Having spoken thus, in the midst of the armies, Arjuna sank on the seat of the chariot, casting away his bow and arrow; heartbroken with grief.

Thus, in the Holy Book the Bhagavad Gita, one of the Upanishads, in the Science of the Supreme Spirit, in the Art of Self-Knowledge, in the colloquy between the Divine Lord Shri Krishna and the Prince Arjuna, stands the first chapter, entitled: The Despondency of Arjuna.

2

明辨之理：數論瑜伽

The Philosophy of Discrimination: Samkhya Yoga

在看到阿朱納的灰心喪志後，作為阿朱納的靈性導師，克里希納開始對阿朱納做了一連串有關人生與宇宙奧秘的開示。這一章的附標題雖是數論瑜伽，但實際上可說是整部《薄伽梵歌》的概論。克里希納在這一章中揭示，我們的身體、身外之世界，以及所有的身體與情緒的感受等，都是造化之幻象；我們的本來面目——自性，也就是聖靈——才是永恆的。因此，我們應善盡此俗世之職責，既不冀求也不迴避；並且應超越所有的苦樂成敗，以無執著之心為之。

本章最後的十八節（2:55-2:72）是《薄伽梵歌》最常被引用的句子。甘地認為這些詩句是《薄伽梵歌》的精華：即使其他詩文都遺失了，光是這幾句詩文就足以教導人如何過一個圓滿的生活。

1. 山佳亞接著敘述：克里希納看著眼中噙著淚水、灰心喪志、被情感淹沒的阿朱納，安慰他，

2. 主道：「我的摯友！值此戰鬥之際，何以屈服於軟弱呢？這對自稱為雅利安者，一點用處也沒有，僅僅是為自己招致罵名，為進入天堂之門設下欄柵。[1]

3.「阿朱納啊！為何臣服於怯懦？你可是令敵人聞而喪膽的人啊！且拋開這些令人難堪的兒女情長，準備就列吧！」

4. 阿朱納辯道：「我的主！我豈能在激戰中，將箭矢送向我當尊敬的毗濕摩與德羅那呢？

5.「我寧願如乞丐般稽首乞憐，也不願殺害我這些有著高雅靈魂的老師們。殺害這些有恩於我的師父們，豈非無異於以他們的血來玷污生命中之甜美歡樂？

6.「我已說不清到底是任由他們征服我，還是由我征服他們較好，若殺了如今備戰中的持國子嗣們，我也將不願苟活。

---

1 歷史學家認為印度的文化來源有二：一是原有以農耕為主的印度河文化，而另一則是約於西元前2000-1500年間自中亞入侵的雅利安文化。雅利安人原為中亞高加索以遊牧為主的印歐人。歷史學家認為印歐人的一支遷入歐洲；而另一支則進入伊朗，稱為「印伊人」（India-Iranian），印伊人後來又進入印度成為雅利安人。雅利安人進入印度後，成為統治階級，也將吠陀經典帶入印度，而後與印度的本土信仰結合而衍生出後來的婆羅門教與印度教。雅利安人（Aryan）源自梵文的 arya，原是高貴、榮耀之意。印度的梵文、伊朗的波斯文，與歐洲的拉丁文均屬印歐語系家族。

1. Sanjaya then told how the Lord Shri Krishna, seeing Arjuna overwhelmed with compassion, his eyes dimmed with flowing tears and full of despondency, consoled him:

The Lord said:

2. My beloved friend! Why yield, just on the eve of battle, to this weakness which does no credit to those who call themselves Aryans, and only brings them infamy and bars against them the gates of heaven?

3. O Arjuna! Why give way to unmanliness? O you who are the terror of your enemies! Shake off such shameful effeminacy, make ready to act!

Arjuna argued:

4. My Lord! How can I, when the battle rages, send an arrow through Bhishma and Drona, who should receive my reverence?

5. Rather would I content myself with a beggar's crust than kill these teachers of mine, these precious noble souls! To slay these masters who are my benefactors would be to stain the sweetness of life's pleasures with their blood.

6. Nor can I say whether it were better that they conquer me or for me to conquer them, since I would no longer care to live if I killed these sons of Dhritarashtra, now preparing for fight.

7. 「我的心有悲憫重擔，而我也因分不清職責之所在。因此，主啊，請告訴我怎麼做對我的靈性福祉最好，因我是您的徒弟。請指引我，我祈求您。

8. 「因為即便獲取這個有形世界的政權，甚或包括無形世界的政權，也無法消除此刻正令我全身麻痺的極度痛苦。」

9. 山佳亞續言道：王啊！這位所向無敵的征服者阿朱納，於是就告訴萬物之主他不戰了，然後緘默不語。

10. 爾時面帶慈祥微笑的主，對著身處兩軍之間、鬱鬱不樂的阿朱納道出如下話語。

11. 克里希納說道：「為何為不值得悲傷者而悲傷，還自言聰慧？智者既不為死者悲，也不為生者悲。

12. 「過去從未有時是我、你，或是這些王子們是不存在的；即使是未來也不會有所改變。

13. 「猶如靈魂居此肉身經歷幼年、壯年與老年，終究它也會換到另一具身體。智者對此未曾有惑。

14. 「身外之冷熱悲喜，來來去去，無一永恆。王子啊！勇敢承受這一切吧！

7. My heart is oppressed with pity; and my mind confused as to what my duty is. Therefore, my Lord, tell me what is best for my spiritual welfare, for I am Your disciple. Please direct me, I pray.

8. For should I attain the monarchy of the visible world, or over the invisible world, it would not drive away the anguish which is now paralyzing my senses.

Sanjaya continued:

9. Arjuna, the conqueror of all enemies, then told the Lord of All-Hearts that he would not fight, and became silent, O King!

10. Thereupon the Lord, with a gracious smile, addressed him who was so much depressed in the midst between the two armies.

Lord Shri Krishna said:

11. Why grieve for those for whom no grief is due, and yet profess wisdom? The wise grieve neither for the dead nor for the living.

12. There was never a time when I was not, nor thou, nor these princes were not; there will never be a time when we shall cease to be.

13. As the soul experiences in this body infancy, youth and old age, so finally it passes into another. The wise have no delusion about this.

14. Those external relations which bring cold and heat, pain and happiness, they come and go; they are not permanent. Endure them bravely, O Prince!

15.「勇者不為境遷，泰然接受苦樂，唯有如此才能堪為不朽。

16.「不存在的（不真實的），永不成真；而存在的（真實的），
也未曾成為虛妄；對於智者而言，這些真理不言自明。[2]

17.「聖靈遍及我們所見的一切，是不滅的，沒有任何東西可
毀滅聖靈。

18.「聖靈是永恆、不可毀、不可思量的，然則作為其居所的
肉身卻是全然有限的。因此，戰鬥吧，勇者！[4]

19.「認為聖靈會殺，或會被殺，都是無明。聖靈既不殺，也
不被殺。

20.「它無生、無死；過去如是，未來亦如是。聖靈從未出
生、是永生、歷久永續，卻又是最古老的；肉體死時，聖
靈不隨之死亡。

21.「知曉聖靈為不可毀、不死、不生、亙古不變者，怎會去
殺或被殺呢？

22.「正如人會拋掉破舊衣袍、換上新衣，同樣聖靈也丟棄破
舊肉身，換上新的肉身。

---

2 原英譯的直譯是：「非」者不會成「是」；「是」者永不成「非」。這裡，「不存在」的，
指的是造化之一切，而「存在」的，則是永恆的聖靈，也就是菩薩薩、自性。在意義
上，這句話與《奇蹟課程》開宗明義的一句話：「凡是真實的，不受任何威脅；凡是不
真實的，根本就不存在。上主的平安即在其中」，意趣相同。
4 這裡「聖靈」指的是大我、自性、真如、佛性，抑或稱之本來面目，皆可。

15. The hero whose soul is unmoved by circumstance, who accepts pleasure and pain with equanimity, only he is fit for immortality.

16. That which is not, shall never be; that which is, shall never cease to be. To the wise, these truths are self-evident.[3]

17. The Spirit, which pervades all that we see, is imperishable. Nothing can destroy the Spirit.

18. The material bodies which this Eternal, Indestructible, Immeasurable Spirit inhabits are all finite. Therefore fight, O Valiant Man!

19. He who thinks that the Spirit kills, and he who thinks of it as killed, are both ignorant. The Spirit kills not, nor is it killed.

20. It was not born; It will never die, nor once having been, can It ever cease to be. Unborn, Eternal, Ever-enduring, yet Most Ancient, the Spirit dies not when the body is dead.

21. He who knows the Spirit as Indestructible, Immortal, Unborn, Always-the-Same, how should he kill or cause to be killed?

22. As a man discards his threadbare robes and puts on new, so the Spirit throws off Its worn-out bodies and takes fresh ones.

---

3 希瓦南達譯文: The unreal has no being; there is no non-being of the Real; the truth about both has been seen by the knowers of the Truth.

23.「武器不可摧之、火不能灼之、水無法淹之，風也不能乾之。

24.「它刀槍不入，水無法淹之、火無法燒之，風也無法乾之。它是永恆、無所不在、不變、不移，且是最古老的。

25.「名之為微不可見（未顯化）、不可思議、亙古不變。得以如此認知聖靈，你就無理由悲傷。

26.「即使你認為它總是不斷生生死死，壯士啊，你仍沒有理由悲傷。

27.「因為有生必有死，正如有死必有生。因此，無須為不可避免之事悲傷。

28.「生命之終始不可知。我們但見其間之起落，故何悲之有？

29.「乍聞聖靈之名，有訝異者，有驚嘆者，也有莫衷所云者。[5] 故聞之者雖眾，但知之者稀矣。

30.「無須為這些將士憂心。人內在之聖靈是不滅的。

31.「你應善盡你的職責。對兵士而言，沒有比一場正義之戰更適得其所的了。因此，阿朱納，無須猶豫不決。

5　這句話頗有《道德經》第四十一章：「上士聞道，勤而行之；中士聞道，若存若亡；下士聞道，大笑之。不笑不足以為道」之意味。

23. Weapons cleave It not, fire burns It not, water drenches It not, and wind dries It not.

24. It is impenetrable; It can be neither drowned nor scorched nor dried. It is Eternal, All-pervading, Unchanging, Immovable and Most Ancient.

25. It is named the Unmanifest, the Unthinkable, the Immutable. Wherefore, knowing the Spirit as such, you have no cause to grieve.

26. Even if you think of it as constantly being born, constantly dying, even then, O Mighty Man! you still have no cause to grieve.

27. For death is as sure for that which is born, as birth is for that which is dead. Therefore grieve not for what is inevitable.

28. The end and beginning of beings are unknown. We see only the intervening formations. Then what cause is there for grief?

29. One hears of the Spirit with surprise, another thinks It marvelous, the third listens without comprehending. Thus, though many are told about It, scarcely is there one who knows It.

30. Be not anxious about these armies. The Spirit in man is imperishable.

31. You must look at your duty. Nothing can be more welcome to a soldier than a righteous war. Therefore to waver in your resolve is unworthy, O Arjuna!

32.「得到機會的兵士是有福的。此機會已為你開啟天堂之門。

33.「大義當前而不戰，你將成為叛徒，失去名譽，徒然為自己招來罪業。

34.「人們將在萬年之後，仍然談論你的恥辱；而不名之譽對於高貴者而言，尤甚於死。

35.「將領們將認為你因懦弱而逃離戰場。儘管過去曾享榮譽，你將遭鄙視。

36.「你的敵人將散佈你的醜聞、嘲笑你的怯懦。還有什麼比這個還更羞辱的呢？

37.「若死，你將上天堂；若勝，則安享俗世之王國。因此昆蒂之子啊，起而戰鬥吧！

38.「平等看待苦樂成敗。準備好作戰，你將不會招致罪業。

39.「我已告訴你知識之道。現在且聽我解釋行動之道。阿朱納，透過此道，你將破除所有行動的束縛。[6]

40.「在此道路上，努力永遠不會白費，也不會被扼殺。即使只有少許修持，也能使人免於大禍。

41.「透過它，紛亂的心智會安立於單一對象的沉思上。相對的，猶豫不決的心智則迷失在無數的羊腸小徑中。

6　知識之道指的是闍那瑜伽，而行動之道則是羯磨瑜伽；兩者分別是第四章與第三章的主題。

32. Blessed are the soldiers who find their opportunity. This opportunity has opened for you the gates of heaven.

33. Refuse to fight in this righteous cause, and you will be a traitor, lost to fame, incurring only sin.

34. Men will talk forever of your disgrace; and to the noble, dishonor is worse than death.

35. Great generals will think that you have fled from the battlefield through cowardice; though once honored you will seem despicable.

36. Your enemies will spread scandal and mock at your courage. Can anything be more humiliating?

37. If killed, you shall attain heaven; if victorious, enjoy the kingdom of earth. Therefore arise, O son of Kunti! and fight.

38. Look upon pleasure and pain, victory and defeat, with an equal eye. Make ready for the combat, and you shall commit no sin.

39. I have told you the philosophy of Knowledge. Now listen and I will explain the philosophy of Action, by means of which, O Arjuna, you shall break through the bondage of all actions.

40. On this Path, endeavor is never wasted, nor can it ever be repressed. Even a very little of its practice protects one from great danger.

41. By its means, the straying intellect becomes steadied in the contemplation of one object only; whereas the minds of the irresolute stray into bypaths innumerable.

42.「唯有無明者才會言詞華麗。正是這樣的人讚美著經文道：『再也沒有比這更深奧的了。』」

43.「他們只聽從欲望的驅使，建造自己的天堂，並設計艱巨繁複的儀軌來確保自身的快樂與權力；如此的唯一結果是再次輪迴投胎。

44.「他們心中充斥著權力與個人享樂的念頭，而無法將其辨識力專注於一點上。

45.「根據吠陀經文所述，生命的組成要素有三，即造化三性。阿朱納啊！提升並超越它們，超越所有二元對立的感受，安立於真理，自世俗的紛擾中解放，並且中定（專注）於自性（大我）之中。[7]

46.「對於了悟自性（大我）的經師而言，吠陀經文的用處，有如水庫之於已然氾濫的地方一般。[8]

47.「你有工作的權利，而無享有成果的權利。勿讓行動的成果成為你的動機，也勿執迷於不行動。

7　廣義的吠陀是古印度宗教與文學作品的總稱，狹義的吠陀則只指四吠陀，亦即《吠陀本集》，包括《梨俱吠陀》（*Rig Veda*）、《娑摩吠陀》（*Sama Veda*）、《夜柔吠陀》（*Yajur Veda*），與《阿闥婆吠陀》（*Atharva Veda*）。 另，關於造化三性的討論，詳見第三章與第十四章。

8　這裡譯者參考了幾個版本，最後採用希瓦南達與伊斯瓦蘭等人的譯文。因為普羅希原譯的中譯是：「正如人可就杯子的任一邊飲水，熟練的經師也可依其自身之目的去曲解經文。」（Purohit: As a man can drink water from any side of a full tank, so the skilled theologian can wrest from any scripture that which will serve his purpose.）但譯者認為，這裡的含意是指當了悟了自性、大我或上帝，訴諸文字之經文就沒有價值了。正如佛陀的筏寓：「法尚應捨，何況非法？」

42. Only the ignorant speak in figurative language. It is they who extol the letter of the scriptures, saying, 'There is nothing deeper than this.'

43. Consulting only their desires, they construct their own heaven, devising arduous and complex rites to secure their own pleasure and their own power; and the only result is rebirth.

44. While their minds are absorbed with ideas of power and personal enjoyment, they cannot concentrate their discrimination on one point.

45. The Vedic Scriptures tell of the three constituents of life – the Qualities. Rise above all of them, O Arjuna! above all the pairs of opposing sensations; be steady in truth, free from worldly anxieties, and centered in the Self.

46. To the Brahmana who has known the Self, all the Vedas are of as much as use as is a reservoir of water in a place where there is a flood.

47. But you have only the right to work, but none to the fruit thereof. Let not then the fruit of your action be your motive; nor yet be enamored of inaction.

48.「不論做什麼事,心念要專注於上帝、放下執著,並同等看待成敗。靈性(瑜伽)即意味著泰然平靜。[9]

49.「肉身的行動遠劣於理智專注於至上。你當仰賴於純然理智。唯有眼光短淺者才會為報償而工作。[10]

50.「一個人一旦證得純然理性,他就棄絕了此俗世之果,不論是善果或惡果。堅持於正行(正確行動)吧。靈性(瑜伽)乃真正的生活藝術。

51.「聖哲們依純然理智的引導,棄絕了行動的果實,並自輪迴的鎖鍊中解脫;他們達到至福之境。

52.「當你的理性跨越了幻象的糾葛,你將對曾聽聞與未曾聽聞的道理,無有分別。

53.「倘若你的理智為各種神聖的經文所困惑,仍能毫不騷動地安立於對『無限』的至福沉思中,那麼你已證得靈性(自我了悟)之境。」[11]

54. 阿朱納問:「主啊!我們怎麼認出誰是已證得純然理智的聖人,誰已臻至至福之境,以及誰的心念是靜定的?他的言行以及生活是如何的呢?」

----

9 普羅希以靈性一詞取代瑜伽(Yoga)。在梵文中,瑜伽原有「合一」的意思。
10 這裡的純然理智即數論中的菩提智。
11「無限」是上帝的同義詞。這裡普羅希將「三摩地」(Samadhi)譯為「對『無限』的至福沉思」。

48. Perform all your actions with mind concentrated on the Divine, renouncing attachment and looking upon success and failure with an equal eye. Spirituality implies equanimity.

49. Physical action is far inferior to an intellect concentrated on the Divine. Have recourse then to Pure Intelligence. It is only the petty-minded who work for reward.

50. When a man attains to Pure Reason, he renounces in this world the results of good and evil alike. Cling to Right Action. Spirituality is the real art of living.

51. The sages guided by Pure Intellect renounce the fruit of action; and, freed from the chains of rebirth, they reach the highest bliss.

52. When your reason has crossed the entanglements of illusion, then shall you become indifferent both to the philosophies you have heard and to those you may yet hear.

53. When the intellect, bewildered by the multiplicity of holy scripts, stands unperturbed in blissful contemplation of the Infinite, then have you attained Spirituality.

Arjuna asked:

54. My Lord! How can we recognize the saint who has attained Pure Intellect, who has reached this state of Bliss, and whose mind is steady? How does he talk, how does he live, and how does he act?

55. 克里希納回答：「當人拋棄了心中的欲望，並全然滿足於自性（大我），他就確然已成就最高境界。

56. 「於苦中心保平靜、於樂中欲望不興，不執著於瞋怒與畏懼，這樣的聖哲就是身處高等境界。

57. 「不論身處何地，或與何人相處，都不會有所執著眷戀；善惡都接受，對人也無好惡，這樣的人就是融入於『無限』之中。

58. 「自外界感官對象的吸引中，收攝自己的感官，猶如烏龜將四肢收回殼中一般，這樣的人已證得圓滿成就。

59. 「對自我節制的人而言，儘管冀求的欲望仍在，但感官的對象已離他而去；對已見到真理的人來說，則是連這些感官的欲求都完全消失了。

60. 「阿朱納啊！儘管人努力嘗試克服，但紛亂的感官仍粗暴地迷亂他的心。[12]

61. 「抑制所有的感官，堅定地沉思於我，如是戰勝感官者終將達於圓滿之境。

62. 「心念繫於感官對象，就會為之所吸引；吸引力發展成為欲望，而欲望則滋養了瞋怒。

---

12 這裡的「心」（mind）即數論中的 manas。

Lord Shri Krishna replied:

55. When a man has given up the desires of his heart and is satisfied with the Self alone, be sure that he has reached the highest state.

56. The sage, whose mind is unruffled in suffering, whose desire is not roused by enjoyment, who is without attachment, anger or fear – take him to be one who stands at that lofty level.

57. He who, wherever he goes, is attached to no person and to no place by ties of flesh; who accepts good and evil alike, neither welcoming the one nor shrinking from the other – take him to be one who is merged in the Infinite.

58. He who can withdraw his senses from the attraction of their objects, as the tortoise draws his limbs within its shell – take it that such a one has attained Perfection.

59. The objects of sense turn from him who is abstemious. Even the relish for them is lost in him who has seen the Truth.

60. O Arjuna! The mind of him who is trying to conquer it is forcibly carried away in spite of his efforts, by his tumultuous senses.

61. Restraining them all, let him meditate steadfastly on Me; for who thus conquers his senses achieves perfection.

62. When a man dwells on the objects of sense, he creates an attraction for them; attraction develops into desire, and desire breeds anger.

63.「嗔怒引發妄念，妄念引發失憶；由於失憶，理性將受損，而理性的喪失將導致毀滅。[13]

64.「但克己自制的靈魂，處於感官對象中，既不執著，也不嫌惡，他贏得永恆的平安。

65.「得平安，則免於不幸，因為心得平安，就能正確明辨。

66.「無法專注者，不能有正確明辨。無法專注，就無法靜坐冥想；無法靜坐，必無法希冀平安；而沒有平安，人怎麼會有幸福呢？

67.「正如海中船隻因暴風雨而翻騰，理性也因心智被逸散的感官所奪而迷喪。

68.「因此，大力士啊！能將感官自其對象抽離者，其理性已然淨化。

69.「當世人沉睡時，唯聖人獨醒；對於世人憑藉以為生者，他不以為意。[14]

70.「猶如川河入海而海水仍不滿溢，平安者的心靈也不因欲望而有所妄動；但欲望充斥者則不然。

----

13 這裡的理性也是指菩提智。

14 這裡多數譯文的直譯是：「對眾生而言的夜晚，自制的聖者是醒著的，但對眾生而言是醒著的白日，則是聖哲眼中的夜晚。」（Sivananda: That which is night to all beings, then the self-controlled man is awake; when all beings are awake, that is night for the sage who sees.）這裡，眾生的夜晚當指自性，因為自性對其而言，陌生有如黑暗之夜晚。而對眾生而言是醒著的白日，是指眾生肉眼所見的物質世界，在聖哲言中則是虛幻不實，猶如夜晚。

63. Anger induces delusion; delusion, loss of memory; through loss of memory, reason is shattered; and loss of reason leads to destruction.

64. But the self-controlled soul, who moves among sense objects, free from either attachment or repulsion, he wins eternal peace.

65. Having attained peace, he becomes free from misery; for when the mind gains peace, right discrimination follows.

66. Right discrimination is not for him who cannot concentrate. Without concentration, there cannot be meditation; he who cannot meditate must not expect peace; and without peace, how can anyone expect happiness?

67. As a ship at sea is tossed by the tempest, so the reason is carried away by the mind when preyed upon by straying senses.

68. Therefore, O Mighty-in-Arms! he who keeps his senses detached from their objects – take it that his reason is purified.

69. The saint is awake when the world sleeps, and he ignores that for which the world lives.

70. He attains peace, into whom desires flow as rivers into the ocean, which though brimming with water remains ever the same; not he whom desire carries away.

71.「摒棄欲望，無所冀求地活於世間，不擁有任何他稱之為
自己財產的事物，且無有驕傲，這樣的人達於平安之境。

72.「阿朱納啊！這就是自性（大我），也就是無上聖靈（梵）
的境界。人一旦達到此境界，就永遠不會失去。即使是臨
命終時，他仍將穩立此境，並將與永恆合一。」[15]

這就是聖靈的科學與自我認識的藝術、奧義書之一的聖
典——《薄伽梵歌》中，克里希納與阿朱納王子對話的第二
章，名為「明辨之理：數論瑜伽」。

15「與永恆合一」原指無上涅槃（Brahma-nirvana）——有限的小我（自我）如蠟燭般消解，
融入於無限永恆的至上。

71. He attains peace who, giving up desire, moves through the world without aspiration, possessing nothing which he can call his own, and free from pride.

72. O Arjuna! This is the state of the Self, the Supreme Spirit, to which if a man once attain, it shall never be taken from him. Even at the time of leaving the body, he will remain firmly enthroned there, and will become one with the Eternal.

Thus, in the Holy Book the Bhagavad Gita, one of the Upanishads, in the Science of the Supreme Spirit, in the Art of Self-Knowledge, in the colloquy between the Divine Lord Shri Krishna and the Prince Arjuna, stands the second chapter, entitled: The Philosophy of Discrimination: Samkhya Yoga.

行動之道：羯磨瑜伽

The Path of Action: Karma Yoga

　　克里希納在這章中提到靈性的兩條道路：行動之道（亦即羯磨瑜伽）與智慧之道（也就是闍那瑜伽）；本章談前者，而後者則是下一章的主題。

　　羯磨（karma）一詞常被譯為「業障」，事實上這個詞係指行為、行動。當人們迷失於造化之中，則其任何行為，不論是身、口、意，都必然帶來後續的結果；這是因果的律則，也就是「業力法則」（law of karma）。一般人認為壞的行動才有「業障」，事實上任何行動，不論好壞，都自有其後果，也都是造化用來將我們束縛在三界中生死輪迴的「障礙」。因為這雙重的意義，有些譯者將此詞譯為「行業」（「行動業力」的簡稱），由於「行業」容易與「商業」（business）與「產業」（industry）二詞產生混淆，為避免混淆，在此譯者採用音譯。

　　《奧義書》說：「人依欲而成，因欲而有意向，因意向而有業，因業而有果。」可見追究根源，因果業力係來自欲望、來自對小我的認同（我執）。克里希納說，欲望源自於造化三性之一的熱情（3:37），再透過感官、心與理智的一起運作而摧毀智慧、蒙蔽靈魂（3:40）。克里希納在本章中也說：

　　「正如火被煙霧遮蔽、鏡子為灰塵覆蓋、嬰孩為子宮所包覆，宇宙也是籠罩於欲望之中。」（3:38）

　　克里希納說，行動之道（羯磨瑜伽）就是正確的行為（3:7），也就是正行。正行也稱正業，是佛教重視的八正道

之一；在佛教經典中，正行意指合理的行為，包括不殺生、不偷盜、不邪淫等。但在本章中，克里希納再次強調並不是迴避行動就可以迴避因果業力，因為只要是身在造化中，就會受到造化三性的影響。

譯文中，行動、行為、作為，可視為同義字。另外，我們有時把行動（action）與不行動（inaction）譯為「為」與「無為」，或「動」與「靜」。讀者從經文中不難發現，《薄伽梵歌》中有頗多思維與老子相近。

在稍後的章節中（包括第五、九、十一章），克里希納一再強調唯有將所有行為作為獻祭，供養上帝──時時刻刻專注於上主的無我行為──才是真正的解脫之道；這便是羯磨瑜伽的真正含意。

1. 阿朱納問道：「我的主！假若智慧高於行動，何以您勸我加入這可怕的戰鬥？

2. 「您的話語令我困惑、思慮不清。因此，請告訴我那僅有的、可以無疑地確保我靈性福祉的道路吧！」

3. 克里希納答道：「正如我已說過的，這個世界有一條雙重道路。無罪者啊！對靜坐者而言，那是智慧之道；對於行動者而言，則是行動之道。

4. 「沒有人可藉由摒棄行動而獲取行動上的自由；也沒有人能光靠拒絕行動而臻至圓滿。

5. 「人甚至想在須臾間完全不動都無法做到，因不論其意欲為何，造化三性必然迫使其行動。

6. 「身體如如不動，無有作為，但一心繫念於感官的對象，如此執迷之靈魂只是一個偽善者。

7. 「但阿朱納啊！榮耀歸於那心智能控制其感官者，因為他踏上了修習羯磨瑜伽之道——正行（正確行為）之道，藉此使他能時時處於不執著之境。

8. 「依職責所在去做吧，因為依職責而為優於無為。人如果保持不動，連要維持肉身都不可能。

Arjuna questioned:

1. My Lord! If wisdom is above action, why do you advise me to engage in this terrible fight?

2. Your language perplexes me and confuses my reason. Therefore please tell me the only way by which I may, without doubt, secure my spiritual welfare.

Lord Shri Krishna replied:

3. In this world, as I have said, there is a twofold path, O Sinless One! There is the Path of Wisdom for those who meditate and the Path of Action for those who work.

4. No man can attain freedom from activity by refraining from action; nor can one reach perfection by merely refusing to act.

5. He cannot even for a moment remain really inactive, for the Qualities of Nature will compel him to act whether he will or no.

6. Whoever remains motionless, refusing to act, but all the while brooding over sensuous object, that deluded soul is simply a hypocrite.

7. But, O Arjuna! All honor to him whose mind controls his senses, for he is thereby beginning to practice Karma Yoga, the Path of Right Action, keeping himself always unattached.

8. Do your duty as prescribed, for action for duty's sake is superior to inaction. Even the maintenance of the body would be impossible if one remained inactive.

9.「於此世界，人們為行動所束縛——除非將行動作為獻祭。因此，阿朱納啊！以無執著之心為之，僅以獻祭為之。[1]

10.「太初，當上帝以祂自己為獻祭創造眾生，祂對眾生說：『藉由獻祭，你們得以昌榮繁茂，也滿足你們所有的欲望。

11.「『因此，崇拜造化的諸神祇，並讓她們以滋養你來作為回報；藉此相互護持，你將獲得最大的福祉。

12.「『因為得到獻祭供養的造化，將賜予你所能冀求的所有快樂。但只享用她所給予而無回報的人，則是真竊賊。』

13.「享用獻祭後的剩餘食物的聖哲們無有罪業；但僅僅為自己準備菜餚的自私者，餵養給自己的卻只是罪業。

14.「所有的生物都是靠食物而活的產物，食物是由雨水而來的產物，雨水藉由獻祭而來，而獻祭正是行動的最高雅形式。

15.「所有行為的源頭是永不毀滅的無上聖靈，而在獻祭中，無所不在的聖靈將會親臨。

16.「所以如果一個人無助於獻祭之輪的運轉，反而過著罪惡的生活，只是享受感官的滿足，阿朱納啊！這樣的人只是徒然活著。

----

1 獻祭（sacrifice；犧牲）一詞的原意是供養的牲品。在此，是指將行為、活動視為供養上帝的牲品。在佛教中，常謂將身口意供養上帝、佛或上師，其意義即在「無我」：因為所有所思所為皆為上帝或大我（聖靈）所為，非小我所作所為，故能無有執著。

9. In this world people are fettered by action, unless it is performed as a sacrifice. Therefore, O Arjuna! let your acts be done without attachment, as sacrifice only.

10. In the beginning, when God created all beings by the sacrifice of Himself, He said unto them: 'Through sacrifice you can procreate, and it shall satisfy all your desires.

11. Worship the Powers of Nature thereby, and let them nourish you in return; thus supporting each other, you shall attain your highest welfare.

12. For, fed on sacrifice, Nature will give you all the enjoyment you can desire. But whoever enjoys what she gives without returning is, indeed, a robber.'

13. The sages who enjoy the food that remains after the sacrifice is made are freed from all sin; but the selfish who spread their feast only for themselves feed on sin only.

14. All creatures are the product of food, food is the product of rain, rain comes by sacrifice, and sacrifice is the noblest form of action.

15. All action originates in the Supreme Spirit, which is Imperishable, and in sacrificial action the all-pervading Spirit is consciously present.

16. Thus he who does not help the revolving wheel of sacrifice, but instead leads a sinful life, rejoicing in the gratification of his senses, O Arjuna! he breathes in vain.

17.「相反地，靜坐沉思於自性（大我）的靈魂則滿足於侍奉自性（大我），並安住於自性（大我）之內；對他而言，不再有什麼事是需要他去達成的。

18.「為或無為，他皆無所得。其福祉不依藉於俗世眾生之作為。

19.「因此善盡你的職責，不去在意結果，因為盡職而不執著者，將證得無上之境。

20.「迦那卡王等人僅藉由行動，就證得圓滿之境。即使只是為了啟發世人，你也責無旁貸。[2]

21.「因為一位偉大的人不論做什麼，其他的人就會跟著模仿。人們依他所立的準則行事。

22.「阿朱納啊！宇宙中沒有什麼是我被迫去做的，也沒有什麼是我需要去達成的；然而我仍恆常有為。

23.「王子啊！倘若我不是永不止息的行動，那麼人們自當樂於起而效尤。

24.「而且我若無有作為，人類將滅絕；我將令世界陷入渾沌，隨之而來的就是毀滅。

----

2 迦那卡王據傳是古代印度的一位國王與明師，「阿虛塔瓦卡拉之歌」（Ashtavakra Gita）即是紀錄迦那卡王與聖人阿虛塔瓦卡拉的對話。在《薄伽梵歌》中，克里希納指出迦那卡王是藉由修習羯磨瑜伽而達到圓滿成就的。

17. On the other hand, the soul who meditates on the Self is content to serve the Self and rests satisfied within the Self – there remains nothing more for him to accomplish.

18. He has nothing to gain by the performance or non-performance of action. His welfare depends not on any contribution that an earthly creature can make.

19. Therefore do your duty perfectly, without care for the results, for he who does his duty disinterestedly attains the Supreme.

20. King Janaka and others attained perfection through action alone. Even for the sake of enlightening the world, it is your duty to act;

21. For whatever a great man does, others imitate. People conform to the standard which he has set.

22. There is nothing in this universe, O Arjuna! that I am compelled to do, nor anything for Me to attain; yet I am persistently active.

23. For were I not to act without ceasing, O Prince! people would be glad to do likewise.

24. And if I were to refrain from action, the human race would be ruined; I should lead the world to chaos, and destruction would follow.

25.「正如無明者之所為，是因為他們樂於有所作為，阿朱納啊！智者之作為也不應有所執著，而應只在意世人的福祉。

26.「不過智者不應去騷動這些執著於作為的無明者之心智；只要專注於我，以正確態度行事，就可以啟發所有的人效尤。

27.「行動是造化內三性的產物。只有被個人小我迷惑的無明者，才會說：『我是作為者。』[3]

28.「但是壯士啊！正確瞭解三性與行動之關係的人，不會執著於行動，因為他知道所有行動都只是他內在三性的作用與反作用（反應）的結果罷了。

29.「不瞭解三性的人對作為感到興趣。儘管如此，瞭解此真理的智者仍不應去打亂這些不懂的人的心。

30.「因此，將你的行動臣服於我，意念專注於絕對者（大我），將自己從自私中解放出來，不期待報償、心不擾動，起而戰鬥！

31.「總是遵循我的戒律行事、信心堅定，且無有疑慮，這樣的人也都免於行為的束縛。

32.「嘲弄我的話語又不遵行的人是無明的，他們又愚又盲，且自取滅亡。

----

3 這裡的「小我」即數論廿四締中的我執、自我感。

25. As the ignorant act, because of their fondness for action, so should the wise act without such attachment, fixing their eyes, O Arjuna! only on the welfare of the world.

26. But a wise man should not perturb the minds of the ignorant, who are attached to action; let him perform his own actions in the right spirit, with concentration on Me, thus inspiring all to do the same.

27. Action is the product of the Qualities inherent in Nature. It is only the ignorant man who, misled by personal egotism, says: 'I am the doer.'

28. But he, O Mighty One! who understands correctly the relation of the Qualities to action is not attached to the act for he perceives that it is merely the action and reaction of the Qualities among themselves.

29. Those who do not understand the Qualities are interested in the act. Still, the wise man who knows the truth should not disturb the mind of him who does not.

30. Therefore, surrendering your actions unto Me, your thoughts concentrated on the Absolute, free from selfishness and without anticipation of reward, with mind devoid of excitement, begin to fight.

31. Those who act always in accordance with My precepts, firm in faith and without cavilling, they too are freed from the bondage of action.

32. But they who ridicule My word and do not keep it, are ignorant, devoid of wisdom and blind. They seek but their own destruction.

33.「即使是智者也是依其天性行事；的確，眾生皆依其本性行事。強迫他們又有何用呢？

34.「感官對象所引發的愛恨皆自造化而生，不要屈服於這些愛恨的情緒；它們只會阻礙道途。

35.「儘管沒有多少功德，盡自己的責任去做，總比去做別人的要好，儘管後者你做得比較稱心。甚至寧可因此而死亡也還是比較好，因為越俎代庖是充滿危險的。」

36. 阿朱納問道：「我的主！請告訴我，是什麼導致一個人犯罪，甚至是違反其意願而彷彿是被迫去做的呢？」

37. 克里希納說：「是欲望、是嫌惡，二者皆源自熱情（情感）；欲望消耗並腐蝕一切，是人最大的敵人。

38.「正如火被煙霧遮蔽、鏡子為灰塵覆蓋、嬰孩為子宮所包覆，宇宙也是籠罩於欲望之中。

39.「它是智者固有的敵人，智慧之顏因之而暗淡。它如火焰一般，永不厭足。

40.「欲望藉由感官、心與理智而運作；它藉此三者之助而摧毀智慧，並蒙蔽靈魂。

41.「因此，阿朱納啊！首要是控制感官，然後斬斷欲望，因為後者滿是罪業，是知識與智慧的毀滅者。

33. Even the wise man acts in character with his nature; indeed, all creatures act according to their natures. What is the use of compulsion then?

34. The love and hate which are aroused by the objects of sense arise from Nature; do not yield to them. They only obstruct the path.

35. It is better to do your own duty, however lacking in merit, than to do that of another, even though efficiently. It is better to die doing one's own duty, for to do the duty of another is fraught with danger.

Arjuna asked:
36. My Lord! Tell me, what is it that drives a man to sin, even against his will and as if by compulsion?

Lord Shri Krishna said:
37. It is desire, it is aversion, born of passion. Desire consumes and corrupts everything. It is man's greatest enemy.

38. As fire is shrouded in smoke, a mirror by dust and a child by the womb, so is the universe enveloped in desire.

39. It is the wise man's constant enemy; it tarnishes the face of wisdom. It is as insatiable as a flame of fire.

40. It works through the senses, the mind and the reason; and with their help destroys wisdom and confounds the soul.

41. Therefore, O Arjuna! first control your senses and then slay desire, for it is full of sin, and is the destroyer of knowledge and of wisdom.

42.「人們說感官的力量強大，但感官之後還有心，心之後則是理智，而比理智更高超偉大的則是祂——上主。

43.「所以，大力士啊！知曉祂是超越理智的，並且藉由祂的幫助，降伏你個人的我執，消滅你的敵人，也就是欲望——不論這會是一項多麼艱辛的挑戰。」

這就是聖靈的科學與自我認識的藝術、奧義書之一的聖典——《薄伽梵歌》中，克里希納與阿朱納王子對話的第三章，名為「行動之道：羯磨瑜伽」。

42. It is said that the senses are powerful. But beyond the senses is the mind, beyond mind is intellect, and beyond and greater than intellect is He.

43. Thus, O Mighty-in-Arms! knowing him to be beyond the intellect and, by His help, subduing your personal egotism, kill your enemy, Desire, extremely difficult though it be."

Thus, in the Holy Book the Bhagavad Gita, one of the Upanishads, in the Science of the Supreme Spirit, in the Art of Self-Knowledge, in the colloquy between the Divine Lord Shri Krishna and the Prince Arjuna, stands the third chapter entitled: The Path of Action: Karma Yoga.

智慧之道：闍那瑜伽

The Path of Wisdom: Jnana Yoga

　　本章的標題是闍那瑜伽，但克里希納在這章談論的，並不僅限於此；關於闍那瑜伽的內容，事實上也分布在不同的章節（包括第六章）。「闍那」（Jnana）的字面意思是知識（knowledge），所以闍那瑜伽也是知識之道。但這裡所說的知識不是關於世間的知識，而可說是一種「真知」（gnosis），也就是智慧，但又不只是世間的智慧。這種智慧，根據史密斯（1995）所言，「毋寧說是一種直覺式的辨識力，具有轉化力量，最終把能知者轉變成為其所知者」；因此「闍那瑜伽是特別提供給有強烈反省傾向的靈性追求者而設的；它是透過知識而與上帝合一的途徑。」可見闍那瑜伽所說的智慧，是超乎頭腦、心智層次的瞭解，而且是深切地體認到耶穌所說的「與父為一」的全然了知。

　　史密斯進一步說：「知的瑜伽（即闍那瑜伽）據說是通向神性實現（了悟）最短的途徑，也是最陡峭的路。它需要理性與靈性作罕見的結合，因此只適合極少數人。」的確，這是一條容易讓人「誤入歧途」的路——我們很容易因為有了很多的知識，而誤以為自己已然瞭解或了悟，但事實上卻只是頭腦層次的理解。[1]

　　在本章中，克里希納揭示了一項奧秘：祂——菩盧薩——雖然住在所有眾生之中，但也直接以肉體形式顯現於世間，目的是為了維護世界的秩序（4:8）。這是上主無限的愛——儘管瞭解一切皆是造化所為，所有的苦難都是虛妄的，

---

[1]　這就有如佛教的唯識論，或是基督宗教中的神學，如果只是鑽研其學理，不論多麼精微，恐怕也只是白費心力。

但出於對眾生無盡的愛，上主仍示現於塵世，引導眾生自幻夢中甦醒。克里希納更進一步說：

「每當靈性衰退、物欲橫行……我就會轉世降生。」（4:7）

世間的師父（靈性導師）很多，或許也都能帶領徒弟到達某種開悟境界，但直接來自「源頭」的明師，無疑地是具有最大的力量──包括慈悲、愛力與智慧，能帶領徒弟早日「回家」。這樣的信仰似乎是印度教與基督宗教特有的。佛教（尤其是大乘或金剛乘）雖也仰賴佛菩薩或上師的力量，但卻認為眾生的自性與佛菩薩一般無二。坦白說，要去辯論何者為真並沒有實質上的意義。一方面是因為語言文字是有限的，而另一方面，則是因為我們每個人都以自己有限的眼光看世界，所以只能以自己理解所及地去瞭解一位師父。因此更真切的問題或許是：當一位了悟自性的師父站在面前時，我們能認得出來嗎？如果我們為世間的概念與知識蒙蔽，恐怕是上帝站在我們面前也不認得！

闍那瑜伽所說的正是這種明辨的真知，但是這種真知卻不是可透過文字傳達的。克里希納在這章中，除了再次說明我們應超越行為結果的束縛，無有執著外，並強調智慧的力量。不執著，意念專注中定，虛心服侍師父，向師父學習，而且不論是任何形式的行動與作為，都應將之作為獻祭──如此我們將能於自性中尋得智慧。

1. 克里希納說：「此一永恆道理，我曾教予太陽王朝的創立者毗瓦斯旺，毗瓦斯旺傳給法典創立者摩奴，摩奴再傳給甘蔗王！

2. 「聖王們都知曉它，因為那是他們的傳承。然而終究還是在久遠之後，為人們所遺忘。

3. 「我如今所揭示給你的，正是此一相同的古老道途，因為你是我的信徒、我的朋友。這是無上的秘密。」

4. 阿朱納問：「我的主！毗瓦斯旺先您而生，您怎麼能夠把這個道理告訴他？」

5. 克里希納答：「我一直以來，一再轉世；阿朱納啊！你也一樣，只是我知道我的生生世世，但你不知道你的。[2]

6. 「我無起始。雖然我是不朽的，也是所有存在的眾生之主，然而，藉由我自己的意願與力量，我讓自己示現人間。[3]

7. 「每當靈性衰退、物欲橫行，阿朱納啊！我就會轉世降生。

8. 「為了捍衛正義，摧毀邪惡，並建立上帝的國度，我世世代代不斷降生。

---

2 基督徒對這兩節詩文必然會有似曾相識的感覺，因為在《約翰福音》（8:57-58）中，猶太人對耶穌質疑道：「你還沒有五十歲，豈見過亞伯拉罕呢？」；耶穌說：「我實實在在地告訴你們，還沒有亞伯拉罕就有了我。」這不正說明上帝在不同時空、不同文化，以不同形象顯化嗎？

3 這裡「意願與力量」係指摩耶（Maya），也就是幻象的力量。

Lord Shri Krishna said:

1. This imperishable philosophy I taught to Vivasvat, the founder of the Sun-dynasty; Vivasvat gave it to Manu the Lawgiver, and Manu to King Ikshvaku!

2. The Divine Kings knew it, for it was their tradition. Then, after a long time, at last it was forgotten.

3. It is this same ancient Path that I have now revealed to you, since you are My devotee and My friend. It is the supreme secret.

Arjuna asked:

4. My Lord! Vivasvat was born before You; how then can You have revealed it to him?

Lord Shri Krishna replied:

5. I have been born again and again, from time to time; you too, O Arjuna! My births are known to Me, but you know not you own.

6. I have no beginning. Though I am imperishable, as well as Lord of all that exists, yet by My own will and power do I manifest Myself.

7. Whenever spirituality decays and materialism is rampant, then, O Arjuna! I reincarnate Myself.

8. To protect the righteous, to destroy the wicked, and to establish the kingdom of God, I am reborn from age to age.

9.「一個人一旦了悟了有關我的誕生與生命的神聖真理，他就不再轉世；而當他離開此肉身時，他將與我合而為一。

10.「許多人將他們的生命融入於我，自欲望、恐懼與憤怒中解脫，心中總是充滿著我，而且因自我克制的明亮火焰而淨化。

11.「不論人們以什麼方式崇拜我，我都歡迎。不論他們選擇怎樣的道路，那道路最終也會引導他們到我這裡。

12.「追求成功者，崇拜諸神祇；而在此俗世他們的行為帶來即刻的果實。

13.「社會中的四種種姓（智者、兵士、商賈與工人）是我依眾生在造化三性與本能上的不同分布而創立的。我是他們的創立者，儘管我自身是不變而無為的。[4]

14.「我不為我的行為所束縛，也不冀求我的行為帶來的任何成果。可如此了悟我的人，就不會被行動奴役。[5]

15.「我們尋求解脫的祖先，依智慧而行。你也當如此行事，正如我們的先祖一般。

16.「何謂『為』，何謂『無為』？智者亦有所疑惑。但我將為你宣說行為（行動）之道，了知它，你將自免於惡。

---

4 印度的種姓制度將人分成四種階級：婆羅門（僧侶）、剎帝利（武士）、吠舍（平民）與首陀羅（奴隸）。這樣的分類有其歷史背景，而後世許多宗教（包括佛教、錫克教等）與宗教改革者都致力於打破這個種姓階級制度。這裡的翻譯是依據普羅希的英譯。

5 4:14-4:24 這十節詩文，事實上是對前一章羯磨瑜伽（行動之道）的進一步闡釋。

9. He who realizes the divine truth concerning My birth and life is not born again; and when he leaves his body, he becomes one with Me.

10. Many have merged their existence in Mine, being freed from desire, fear and anger, filled always with Me and purified by the illuminating flame of self-abnegation.

11. Howsoever men try to worship Me, so do I welcome them. By whatever path they travel, it leads to Me at last.

12. Those who look for success, worship the Powers; and in this world their actions bear immediate fruit.

13. The four divisions of society (the wise, the soldier, the merchant, the laborer) were created by Me, according to the natural distribution of Qualities and instincts. I am the author of them, though I Myself do no action, and am changeless.

14. My actions do not fetter Me, nor do I desire anything that they can bring. He who thus realizes Me is not enslaved by action.

15. In the light of wisdom, our ancestors, who sought deliverance, performed their acts. You should act also, as did our fathers of old.

16. What is action and what is inaction? It is a question which has bewildered the wise. But I will declare unto you the philosophy of action, and knowing it, you shall be free from evil.

17.「辨明何為正確的行動、何為錯誤的行動,以及何謂不行動(無為),是必要的,因為行為(行動)的法則不可思議。

18.「能見動中之靜、靜中之動者,為上智者。儘管他有所為,仍是聖人。

19.「如此之人,智者稱之為聖哲,因為其所有作為皆非由欲望所驅使;而且其行止也為智慧之火所淨化。

20.「臣服於行動的結果,無有冀求,總是知足而獨立;於此實相,他無所為,儘管他顯然有所為。

21.「無有期待,心無放逸,無有貪欲,僅有身行。儘管有為,心無染著。

22.「滿足地接受所有來到他面前的,心中無有抗拒;超越二元對立,無有欽羨,心不落於成敗;儘管有所作為,但不受結果成敗之束縛。

23.「無有執著,自在,意念中定於智慧,以獻祭之心行事,這樣的人行事不留痕跡。

24.「對他而言,獻祭本身即為聖靈(梵);聖靈(梵)與供養為一;是聖靈(梵)將自己獻祭於自己的火焰之中,而儘管有所為,他與上帝是合一的,因為在行動當中,他的心念始終未曾偏離上帝。

17. It is necessary to consider what is right action, what is wrong action, and what is inaction, for mysterious is the law of action.

18. He who can see inaction in action, and action in inaction, is the wisest among men. He is a saint, even though he still acts.

19. The wise call him a sage; for whatever he undertakes is free from the motive of desire, and his deeds are purified by the fire of wisdom.

20. Having surrendered all claim to the results of his actions, always contented and independent, in reality he does nothing, even though he is apparently acting.

21. Expecting nothing, his mind and personality controlled, without greed, doing bodily actions only – though he acts, yet he remains untainted.

22. Content with what comes to him without effort of his own, mounting above the pairs of opposites, free from envy, his mind balanced both in success and failure – though he acts, yet the consequences do not bind him.

23. He who is without attachment, free, his mind centered in wisdom, his actions, being done as a sacrifice, leave no trace behind.

24. For him, the sacrifice itself is the Spirit; the Spirit and the oblation are one; it is the Spirit itself which is sacrificed in Its own fire, and the man even in action is united with God, since while performing his act, his mind never ceases to be fixed on him.

25. 「一些聖哲將獻祭供養諸神祇，而有些聖哲（已了悟自性者），則以自己為獻祭，供養於永恆者（上帝）的祭壇。

26. 「有些人將身體感官獻祭給克己自制之火；另有一些人則將他們與外界事物的接觸，供養給感官的獻祭之火。[6]

27. 「還有一些人，將其所有活動，包括呼吸的維生功能，獻祭給由智慧所點燃的自我克制的靈性之火。

28. 「另外還有一些人以財富、苦行與靜坐沉思作為獻祭。持戒之僧侶則捨棄其經典修持，甚至是其靈性力量，來作為供養。

29. 「有些人修持生命能量的控制，控制上行氣與下行氣這些細微力量的運作，藉此將上行氣獻祭給下行氣，也把下行氣獻祭給上行氣。[7]

30. 「另有一些人節制飲食，將他們的俗世生命獻祭給靈性之火。所有這些人都瞭解獻祭的主旨；藉由獻祭，他們的罪業都得以洗淨。

----

6 這裡「與外界事物的接觸」係指「色聲香味觸」等外塵，而「身體感官」則是「眼耳鼻舌身」等五知根。

7 印度瑜伽學派之一的哈達瑜伽，就是以呼吸控制、身體鍛鍊等體位法為主的修行方法。呼吸控制法（Pranayama; 或譯「調息法」）是由梵文 Prana 和 Yama 二字所組成，Prana 意為生命的能量，Yama 為控制，所以呼吸控制法就是控制身體內部生命能量的方法。身體內有十種重要的生命能量：Prana、Apana、Samana、Udaha、Vyana、Naga、Kurma、Krkara、Devadatta 和 Dhanainjaya，統稱為 Pranah。其中「上行氣」（Prana）介於肚臍和喉嚨之間，主心臟、肺、呼吸之控制；「下行氣」（Apana）則介於肚臍和肛門之間，主排泄尿液和糞便之控制。參見 http://www.ananda-yoga.org/air.htm。Prana 與 Apana 也分別有吸收養分與排出廢物的意義；有興趣者可參考 Kaminoff（2007）的《瑜伽解剖書》。

25. Some sages sacrifice to the Powers; others offer themselves on the altar of the Eternal.

26. Some sacrifice their physical senses in the fire of self-control; others offer up their contact with external objects in the sacrificial fire of their senses.

27. Others again sacrifice their activities and their vitality in the spiritual fire of self-abnegation, kindled by wisdom.

28. And yet others offer as their sacrifice wealth, austerities and meditation. Monks wedded to their vows renounce their scriptural learning and even their spiritual powers.

29. There are some who practice control of the vital energy and govern the subtle forces of Prana and Apana, thereby sacrificing their Prana unto Apana, or their Apana unto Prana.

30. Others, controlling their diet, sacrifice their worldly life to the spiritual fire. All understand the principle of sacrifice, and by its means their sins are washed away.

31.「作為獻祭的獎賞,他們得以品嚐不死之甘露,達至永生之境。這個世界不屬於那些不願意獻祭的人;更不用說是其他世界了。

32.「以聖靈故,種種獻祭皆可如此行之。當知所有這些都需仰賴行動。瞭解了這點,你就可得自由。

33. 阿朱納啊!智慧之獻祭優於所有物質之獻祭,因為行動的頂點總歸是了悟。[8]

34.「你應藉由頂禮於師父(靈性導師)腳下、向他請益,並以侍奉他作為學習。了悟真理的智者會將智慧教導予你。

35.「阿朱納啊!瞭解了這一點,你將不再有迷惑;而且藉由此智慧的力量,所有這些人,在你眼中將如同你本身的自性(大我)一般,因此也就如同我一樣。

36.「即使你是罪業深重,你仍將可以依此智慧之筏渡過一切罪業。

37.「阿朱納啊!正如熊熊烈火燒掉燃料,智慧之火焰也將行動之餘火燒成灰燼。

38.「世上有如是淨化力量者,莫過於智慧;而圓滿成就之聖人終將於其自性中尋得智慧。

---

8 這句話頗有《金剛經》所言的「法布施優於財布施」的意味。

31. Tasting the nectar of immortality as the reward of sacrifice, they reach the Eternal. This world is not for those who refuse to sacrifice; much less the other world.

32. In this way other sacrifices too may be undergone for the Spirit's sake. Know that they all depend on action. Knowing this, you shall be free.

33. The sacrifice of wisdom is superior to any material sacrifice, for O Arjuna! the climax of action is always Realization.

34. This shall you learn by prostrating yourself at the Master's feet, by questioning Him and by serving Him. The wise who have realized the Truth will teach you wisdom.

35. Having known that, you shall never again be confounded; and, O Arjuna! by the power of that wisdom, you shall see all these people, as it were, as your own Self, and therefore as Me.

36. Be you the greatest of sinners, yet you shall cross over all sin by the ferryboat of wisdom.

37. As the kindled fire consumes the fuel, so, O Arjuna! in the flame of wisdom the embers of action are burnt to ashes.

38. There is nothing in the world so purifying as wisdom; and he who is a perfect saint finds that at last in his own Self.

39.「信心（道心）滿滿者，證得智慧；而能控制其感官者亦然。既得此智慧，則離證得無上平安之日亦不遠矣。

40.「但無明者、無信心者與懷疑論者則都迷失了。不論是這個世界或是任何其他地方，對於心中總是懷疑的人而言，都是毫無幸福可言的。

41.「然而對為了靜坐沉思而捨棄行動，揮智慧之劍劈開疑慮，且始終穩立於自性的人而言，是不被其行動所束縛的。

42.「因此，以智慧之劍破除你心中因無明而起的疑慮，遵循智慧之道，奮起吧！」

這就是聖靈的科學與自我認識的藝術、奧義書之一的聖典——《薄伽梵歌》中，克里希納與阿朱納王子對話的第四章，名為「智慧之道：闍那瑜伽」。

39. He who is full of faith attains wisdom, and he too who can control his senses. Having attained that wisdom, he shall ere long attain the Supreme Peace.

40. But the ignorant man, and he who has no faith, and the skeptic are lost. Neither in this world nor elsewhere is there any happiness in store for him who always doubts.

41. But the man who has renounced his action for meditation, who has cleft his doubt in twain by the sword of wisdom, who remains always enthroned in his Self, is not bound by his acts.

42. Therefore, cleaving asunder with the sword of wisdom the doubts of your heart, which your own ignorance has engendered, follow the Path of Wisdom and arise!

Thus, in the Holy Book the Bhagavad Gita, one of the Upanishads, in the Science of the Supreme Spirit, in the Art of Self-Knowledge, in the colloquy between the Divine Lord Shri Krishna and the Prince Arjuna, stands the fourth chapter entitled: The Path of Wisdom: Jnana Yoga.

5

行為之捨棄

The Renunciation of Action

　　在前一章最後兩句詩文中（4:41-4:42），克里希納談到為了靜坐沉思而捨棄行為的智者，其行為不受束縛；祂因此鼓勵阿朱納遵循智慧之道（闍那瑜伽），以智慧之劍破除無明。這又意味著依智慧之道而捨棄行動也是克里希納所贊同的，但這似乎與羯磨瑜伽所倡導的正行有所牴觸。阿朱納因而在本章中，對此二者間的分別，繼續提出他的疑慮。

　　本章所談的行為之捨棄（也譯作「出離」），也就是印度傳統所說的「桑雅薩」（sannyasa）。印度將人的一生分成四個理想化的階段，即「四住期」：學徒期、家居期、林隱期與棄世期（sannyasa；也譯「雲遊期」）。第一階段始於「印心」（initiation）（也因靈性傳承之不同而譯做「點化」或「灌頂」），也就是接受了師父或老師的認可之後成為徒弟，學習師父傳授的一切。

　　第二階段進入婚姻生活，開始善盡個人的家庭與社會責任。第三階段是當一個人完成了他的家庭社會責任後，進入森林成為隱者，將更大的心力投入靈性修持。

　　到了第四階段，林隱者再次回到社會，但卻不是回到原來的家庭，而是作為苦行者或是托缽僧（稱為「桑雅士」〔sannyasi〕），居無定所；靈性修持仍是其生命重心，但這回卻不是避世，而是某種形式的入世。或許林隱期是外在的捨棄，而棄世期才是真正的捨棄吧！

　　對於阿朱納的問題，克里希納回應說，正行較捨棄行動佳，但實際上卻強調二者是不可分的；重要的是內在，而不是外在的行為。專注、無有執著，將一切作為獻祭獻給至上，則

不論外在是有所為或無為，都能於自性中證得平安，與上主合一。

　　本章最後三句詩文（5:27-5:29）談到靜坐，當可看成是下一章禪定瑜伽的引言。

1. 阿朱納道:「主啊!您時而讚揚捨棄行動,時而稱讚正行(正確行為)。我祈求您,請告訴我何者是真正有助於我的最高福祉呢?」

2. 克里希納答道:「捨棄行動與正行之道,二者皆可使你臻於至境;但二者中,後者較佳。

3. 「無好亦無惡,心不為二元對立所動,並且輕易地自束縛中解脫,這樣的人是真正的苦行者。

4. 「唯有不開悟者才會視智慧與正行(正確行為)二者為迥異之事,智者則不然。然則任何人但且知其一,即可得享二者之果。

5. 「經由智慧所達到的境界,同樣可藉由正行來達成。視二者為一者,是了知真理者。

6. 「壯士啊!沒有專注,捨棄是艱難的。總是靜坐沉思於至聖(上帝)的聖哲,不需長久歲月即可臻至絕對之境。

7. 「屬靈、單純、克服其感官與個人之小我,而且也了悟其至高之自性同樣也是所有眾生的自性,這樣的人,儘管有所為,不會被其行為所束縛。

8. 「聖人雖也看、聽、觸、聞、食、動、睡,以及呼吸,但他瞭解真理,知曉他本人並不是這個作為者。

Arjuna said:

1. My Lord! At one moment You praise renunciation of action; at another, right action. Tell me truly, I pray, which of these is the more conducive to my highest welfare?

Lord Shri Krishna replied:

2. Renunciation of action and the path of right action both lead to the highest; of the two, right action is the better.

3. He is a true ascetic who never desires or dislikes, who is uninfluenced by the opposites and is easily freed from bondage.

4. Only the unenlightened speak of wisdom and right action as separate; not the wise. If any man knows one he enjoys the fruit of both.

5. The level which is reached by wisdom is attained through right action as well. He who perceives that the two are one knows the truth.

6. Without concentration, O Mighty Man! renunciation is difficult. But the sage who is always meditating on the Divine, before long shall attain the Absolute.

7. He who is spiritual, who is pure, who has overcome his senses and his personal self, who has realized his highest Self as the Self of all, such a one, even though he acts, is not bound by his acts.

8. Though the saint sees, hears, touches, smells, eats, moves, sleeps and breathes, yet he knows the Truth, and he knows that it is not he who acts.

9.「他雖也談說，有施受，眼有開闔，但他仍瞭解這只是他的感官嬉戲於其感知的對象罷了。

10.「將所有行動獻給聖靈，完全無個人之執著，這樣的人被罪業所染著的程度，一如蓮花為水所沾濕的程度，微乎其微。

11.「聖哲之作為不帶激情，總是將身、心、理智，甚至是感官，作為其淨化的工具。

12.「棄絕了行為的果實，他贏得了永恆的平安。至於不認識靈性的人，為欲望所驅使，執著於他們所認為的行動所帶來的好處，反而與之糾葛纏結。

13.「打從內心捨棄所有行動作為，克己自制的靈魂於其九竅之城中——也就是此肉身——享得極樂；既無所為，也未引發其他之作為。

14.「宇宙之主並未對行為、因由，或是因緣果報，訂下什麼規則。所有種種，都是造化的運作使然。[1]

15.「上主不為任何人的罪業或福報承擔責任。人們迷惑，是因為其內在之智慧被無明（愚昧）遮掩了。

16.「誠然，智慧就像太陽一般，將無上真理揭示給那些以自性之智慧驅散其無明的人們。

---

1 這裡，克里希納闡述因果法則並不是最高的上帝（道）制訂的。因果法則是造化三界內的律則。

9. Though he talks, though he gives and receives, though he opens his eyes and shuts them, he still knows that his senses are merely disporting themselves among the objects of perception.

10. He who dedicates his actions to the Spirit, without any personal attachment to them, he is no more tainted by sin than the water lily is wetted by water.

11. The sage performs his action dispassionately, using his body, mind and intellect, and even his senses, always as a means of purification.

12. Having abandoned the fruit of action, he wins eternal peace. Others, unacquainted with spirituality, led by desire and clinging to the benefit which they think will follow their actions, become entangled in them.

13. Mentally renouncing all actions, the self-controlled soul enjoys bliss in this body, the city of the nine gates, neither doing anything himself nor causing anything to be done.

14. The Lord of this universe has not ordained activity, or any incentive thereto, or any relation between an act and its consequences. All this is the work of Nature.

15. The Lord does not accept responsibility for any man's sin or merit. Men are deluded because in them wisdom is submerged in ignorance.

16. Surely wisdom is like the sun, revealing the supreme truth to those whose ignorance is dispelled by the wisdom of the Self.

17.「他們靜坐沉思於至聖（上帝）、對至聖有堅定信心（道心）、專注於至聖，並於至聖中失去自我，罪業也於智慧中消解；他們將不再回來。[2]

18.「聖哲們平等看待一切眾生，不論他是學養兼備的僧侶（婆羅門）、是無宗教信仰者，抑或者是牛、象或犬。

19.「心念專注於至上（上帝），始終保持平衡，即使於此俗世，他們仍征服了他們的塵世生命；因為至上（上帝）是既無瑕疵也無偏頗的。

20.「了悟並活於絕對之境，其心不動、不亂；不為樂喜，不為苦悲。

21.「心不冀求與俗世接觸，其自性與永恆合一，這樣的聖哲於其自性中尋得幸福，並享有永恆極樂。

22.「外在關係所帶來的歡樂伴隨著苦痛；這種歡樂有始有終。智者對此不感欣喜。

23.「在離開此肉身前，就學會了不受欲望與嗔怒的鼓動，這樣的人是聖人，而且也是幸福的。

24.「於其自性中自得其樂，並尋得平安，從而使其自性光輝顯露，這樣的聖哲證得永恆極樂，自身成為聖靈。[3]

2　「不再回來」意指解脫，不再需要生死輪迴。

3　這裡所說的「證得永恆極樂」原是指「於梵中證得涅槃」；下一句中「回歸於永恆的聖靈」同此。

17. Meditating on the Divine, having faith in the Divine, concentrating on the Divine and losing themselves in the Divine, their sins dissolved in wisdom, they go whence there is no return.

18. Sages look equally upon all, whether it be a minister of learning and humility or an infidel, or whether it be a cow, an elephant or a dog.

19. Even in this world they conquer their earth-life whose minds, fixed on the Supreme, remain always balanced; for the Supreme has neither blemish nor bias.

20. He who knows and lives in the Absolute remains unmoved and unperturbed; he is not elated by pleasure or depressed by pain.

21. He finds happiness in his own Self and enjoys eternal bliss, whose heart does not yearn for the contacts of earth and whose Self is one with the Everlasting.

22. The joys that spring from external associations bring pain; they have their beginnings and their endings. The wise man does not rejoice in them.

23. He who, before he leaves his body, learns to surmount the promptings of desire and anger, is a saint, and is happy.

24. He who is happy within his Self and has found its peace, and in whom the inner light shines, that sage attains Eternal Bliss and becomes the Spirit itself.

25.「罪業洗淨、分離感消失、征服自我，而且只尋求眾生之福祉，這樣的聖哲回歸於永恆的聖靈。[4]

26.「了悟自性、控制心念，且心中無有欲望與瞋怒，如此之聖人無處不見永恆極樂。

27.「摒除外在事物、凝視於兩眉之間，以鼻調勻呼氣與吸氣；[5]

28.「觀照感官、意念與理智，心念致力於解脫，無有欲望、恐懼與瞋怒，這樣的聖哲得永恆之自由解脫。

29.「了知我是欣然接受所有苦行與獻祭之供養的，是諸世界的強大統治者，而且也是眾生之友，這樣的聖人達到了永恆平安之境。」

這就是聖靈的科學與自我認識的藝術、奧義書之一的聖典——《薄伽梵歌》中，克里希納與阿朱納王子對話的第五章，名為「行為之捨棄」。

4　這裡分離感係指眾生心中與上主分離的感覺；分離感消失就是與上主合一。
5　這兩眉之間即眉心輪，也就是第三眼。

25. Sages whose sins have been washed away, whose sense of separateness has vanished, who have subdued themselves, and seek only the welfare of all, come to the Eternal Spirit.

26. Saints who know their Selves, who control their minds, and feel neither desire nor anger, find Eternal Bliss everywhere.

27. Excluding external objects, his gaze fixed between the eyebrows, the inward and outward breathings passing equally through his nostrils;

28. Governing sense, mind and intellect, intent on liberation, free from desire, fear and anger, the sage is forever free.

29. Knowing Me as Him who gladly receives all offerings of austerity and sacrifice, as the Mighty Ruler of all the worlds and the Friend of all beings, he passes to Eternal Peace.

Thus, in the Holy Book the Bhagavad Gita, one of the Upanishads, in the Science of the Supreme Spirit, in the Art of Self-Knowledge, in the colloquy between the Divine Lord Shri Krishna and the Prince Arjuna, stands the fifth chapter entitled: The Renunciation of Action.

– Chapter –

6

靜坐與克己自制：
禪定瑜伽

**Meditation and Self Control:
Dhyana Yoga**

本章的主題是禪定瑜伽，也就是勝王瑜伽（raja yoga）。史密斯在《世界宗教》中說，在印度勝王瑜伽被認為是「通向重新整合的皇家（raj）之路」，因為「它帶領人到令人目眩的高度（境界）……乃是一條通過身心試驗走向神的路」。為什麼呢？因為根據《奧義書》，「感官是向外的，人們因此朝外面的事物看，而看不到內在的存有。只有少數聰明人對外面的東西閉上眼睛，而看到內在自性的光輝。」

　　本章談禪定瑜伽，但內容與前一章也都有些關連。在前一章中，克里希納雖然告訴阿朱納正行要比捨棄行動佳，但也強調二者是不可分的。在這一章的開頭，祂更直接說捨棄就是正行（6:2）。

　　克里希納接著談論靜坐之道，而這也是前一章最後三節談論的。除了對靜坐的姿勢與場所有簡單的建議外，祂強調我們應克己自制、生活中道，如是持續專注的精進修行，終將會帶來靈性的果實。

　　本章的後半段，阿朱納問及多數修行人會遇到的問題：我們如何降伏紛飛的意念（一如須菩提在《金剛經》中向釋迦牟尼佛請益如何降伏其心）？克里希納建議應持續修持與捨棄（6:35），如此學得克己自制，將終能證得了悟（6:36）；即便無法修習禪定之道，祂也保證只要行正道——儘管偶有過失——就永不墜惡道。

1. 克里希納道：「盡責任而為，不考慮後果者，才是真屬靈與真苦行；僅僅遵行儀軌或迴避行為者，則都不是。

2.「阿朱納啊！事實上，捨棄就是所謂的正行。一個人只要還沒有捨棄所有欲望，就稱不上是屬靈的。

3.「對追求靈性靜坐之境界的聖哲而言，修行是唯一法門，而當他證得這些境界，他仍必須藉由不輟的克己自制來維持其等級。

4.「當一個人連行動的初念都捨棄了，當他對感官對象以及伴隨著行動而來的結果都不感興趣，那麼他是真正地瞭解靈性的真諦了。

5.「他當藉其最高的心靈之協助以求得解脫，且不貶抑他自己的心靈。因為心靈雖是他唯一的朋友；但也可成為他的敵人。[1]

----

1 這裡譯者將普羅希英譯的「Self」譯為「心靈」，因為在此並非指最高的自性、佛性；以下幾節同此。伊斯瓦蘭認為這裡的心靈有意志的意味。事實上，這裡所說的心靈，其梵文原文是「阿特曼」（ātman），只是這個詞同樣有自我、靈魂等各種不同的意思。尤迦南達將之譯為「小我」（self）、「我執」（ego），而認為最高的心靈是所謂的「大我」（Self）、「靈魂」（soul）。我們每個人都生而有各種不同的我執。我執雖然意味著對個人小我的認同，但克里希納在這句經文中指出，我們不應持貶抑的態度來看待我執。因為我執雖使我們與上帝「隔離」，但沒有我執，我們也無法修行（真可謂「成也我執，敗也我執」）。《薄伽梵歌》中一再強調我們應泰然平等地看待來來去去的各種情緒、欲望與我執，因為這些都不是我們的真正本來面目（大我、自性）。我們如果貶抑了某個小我，代表的是我們對另一個批判的小我的認同。因此重點是我們面對我執的態度。

Lord Shri Krishna said:

1. He who acts because it is his duty, not thinking of the consequences, is really spiritual and a true ascetic; and not he who merely observes rituals or who shuns all action.

2. O Arjuna! Renunciation is in fact what is called Right Action. No one can become spiritual who has not renounced all desires.

3. For the sage who seeks the heights of spiritual meditation, practice is the only method, and when he has attained them, he must maintain himself there by continual self-control.

4. When a person renounces even the thought of initiating action, when he is not interested in sense objects or any results which may flow from his acts, then in truth he understands spirituality.

5. Let him seek liberation by the help of his highest Self, and let him never disgrace his own Self. For that Self is his only friend; yet it may also be his enemy.

6.「對藉由心靈之助而克服低等天性的人而言，心靈是朋友；但對於未能如是者而言，心靈是敵人。[2]

7.「對克己自制、已證得平安之境者而言，其心靈不為冷熱、苦樂、榮辱所動。

8.「心中只冀求智慧與靈性的洞見、克服感官，而且看待黃金與糞土無二，這樣的人是真聖人。

9.「不偏頗地看待所有的人——不論是愛人、朋友或敵人，是冷漠者或心懷敵意者，也不論親疏、善惡。

10.「靈性修持者當不懈怠地練習集中意念，過隱退避靜生活，孑然一身，控制意念與品行，無有欲望、無有財物。

11.「選定一處聖所後，當以堅定姿勢坐於座上，座位不太高也不太低，上面鋪上草席、鹿皮與布。

12.「如是坐定，意念專注，收攝身體機能與觀照感官；他當如是修持靜坐冥想以淨化其低等天性。

13.「他當保持身體如如不動、頭頸端正，正正凝視鼻尖，不偏左也不偏右。[3]

2　這裡，低等天性當指機械性、惰性的品質。

3　有些譯注者認為這裡所說的「凝視鼻尖」是指專注于兩眉之間的眉心輪，不過有些靜坐法（如蔣維喬所提倡的「因是子靜坐法」）認為凝視鼻尖可使精神振作，治昏沉。

6. To him who has conquered his lower nature by its help, the Self is a friend, but to him who has not done so, it is an enemy.

7. The Self of him who is self-controlled and has attained peace is equally unmoved by heat or cold, pleasure or pain, honor or dishonor.

8. He who desires nothing but wisdom and spiritual insight, who has conquered his senses and who looks with the same eye upon a lump of earth, a stone or fine gold, is a real saint.

9. He looks impartially on all – lover, friend or foe; indifferent or hostile; alien or relative; virtuous or sinful.

10. Let the student of spirituality try unceasingly to concentrate his mind; let him live in seclusion, absolutely alone, with mind and personality controlled, free from desire and without possessions.

11. Having chosen a holy place, let him sit in a firm posture on a seat, neither too high nor too low, and covered with a grass mat, a deer skin and a cloth.

12. Seated thus, his mind concentrated, its functions controlled and his senses governed, let him practice meditation for the purification of his lower nature.

13. Let him hold body, head and neck erect, motionless and steady; let him look fixedly at the tip of his nose, turning neither to the right nor to the left.

14.「心保平靜，無有畏懼，遵守獨身誓言，控制意念並專注於大我，他當在沉思於大我中失去自我。[4]

15.「如此意念恆常與我交流，念頭降伏，他將證得平安之境；此平安之境來自於我，而且終將為他帶來解脫。

16.「靜坐沉思並不是給吃太多或什麼也不吃的人，同樣也不是給耽溺於睡眠或總是醒著的人。

17.「但對於節制飲食與娛樂，而且於行住坐臥都保持中道的人而言，靜坐將會驅離所有的痛苦。

18.「當完全控制住意念，中定於自性，且無有任何塵世之欲望，那麼此人是真屬靈的。

19.「戰勝意念並融入於自性的智者，有如一盞屹立不搖的燈，因它有遮蔽，不為四方的風所動。

20.「於此，一切天性，不論高低，皆為自性光所悉見；人將安住於自性之中，享有滿足；藉著與至聖的合一，身體機能收攝了，心靈也尋得安息。

21.「當他得享那只有純然理智才能捕捉而又超越感官的極樂，當他安息於其至高之自性中，他將永遠不再偏離實相。

---

4 「失去自我」是消除對小我的認同，而融入於無分別的大我中；莊子所說的「坐忘」，大概也是這樣的境界。

14. With peace in his heart and nor fear, observing the vow of celibacy, with mind controlled and fixed on Me, let the student lose himself in contemplation of Me.

15. Thus keeping his mind always in communion with Me, and with his thoughts subdued, he shall attain that Peace which is Mine and which will lead him to liberation at last.

16. Meditation is not for one who eats too much, nor for one who eats not at all; nor for one who is overmuch addicted to sleep, nor for one who is always awake.

17. But for one who regulates food and recreation, who is balanced in action, in sleep and in waking, it shall dispel all unhappiness.

18. When the mind, completely controlled, is centered in the Self, and free from all earthly desires, then is a person truly spiritual.

19. The wise man who has conquered his mind and is absorbed in the Self is as a lamp which does not flicker, since it stands sheltered from every wind.

20. There, where the whole nature is seen in the light of the Self, where the person abides within his Self and is satisfied, there, its functions restrained by its union with the Divine, the mind finds rest.

21. When he enjoys the bliss which passes sense, and which only the Pure Intellect can grasp, when he comes to rest within his own highest Self, never again will he stray from reality.

22.「一旦尋得，他將了悟再也沒有如此珍貴的寶藏了。而且一旦得到，就再也沒有任何災禍可以擾動得了他。

23.「如此從內在根本去切斷苦難的折磨，即是靈性（瑜伽），而這有賴於以決心與不屈不撓之心行之。

24.「棄絕所有想像得到的欲望，時時刻刻以意志的力量控制感官。

25.「一點一滴，藉由堅定理智的協助，如此當可證得平安之境；而且，應當將意念專注於自性，此外別無所思。

26.「當心猿意馬、意念紛飛，應抑止它，並讓它再次回歸心靈，成為擁護自性的一員。

27.「意念平和、熱情止息、無有罪業，且與絕對者（上帝）合一的聖哲，無上的喜悅是屬於他的。

28.「無有罪業，恆常安住於永恆之境，如此之聖人無需費力即享有經由了悟無限者（上帝）而得來的無上喜樂。

29.「證得生命之一統性者，於眾生中見到其自性，也在其自性中見到眾生，而且能以不偏頗的眼光看待萬物。

30.「能在萬物中看到我，而且也能在我中看到萬物，這樣的人我永遠不會離棄，而他也永不會失去我。[5]

5　「在萬物中看到我」意指在有限的萬物中，都看到其內的上帝本質；「在我中看到萬物」則是看到上帝的無限。耶穌與莊子都說過類似的話語。耶穌說：「我就是在萬物之上的光。我就是一切：一切從我而來，一切回歸於我。劈一塊木材，我就在那裡。舉起一塊

22. Finding That, he will realize that there is no possession so precious. And when once established there, no calamity can disturb him.

23. This inner severance from the affliction of misery is spirituality. It should be practiced with determination and with a heart which refuses to be depressed.

24. Renouncing every desire which imagination can conceive, controlling the senses at every point by the power of mind;

25. Little by little, by the help of his reason controlled by fortitude, let him attain peace; and, fixing his mind on the Self, let him not think of any other thing.

26. When the volatile and wavering mind would wander, let him restrain it and bring it again to its allegiance to the Self.

27. Supreme bliss is the lot of the sage, whose mind attains Peace, whose passions subside, who is without sin, and who becomes one with the Absolute.

28. Thus, free from sin, abiding always in the Eternal, the saint enjoys without effort the bliss which flows from realization of the Infinite.

29. He who experiences the unity of life sees his own Self in all beings and all beings in his own Self, and looks on everything with an impartial eye;

30. He who sees Me in everything and everything in Me, him shall I never forsake, nor shall he lose Me.

31.「了悟生命之一統性，並崇拜萬物中的我，這樣的聖哲不論境遇為何，總是活在我裡面。

32.「阿朱納啊！不論外在形勢是苦是樂，處處皆能從中看到與其內在相同的自性，這樣的人是完美的聖人。」

33. 阿朱納道：「由於我心念不定，我不知如何能達到您所揭示的這種泰然境界。

34.「主啊！確然，心念變幻無常、頑冥不化，且又如風一般非常難以駕馭。」

35. 克里希納答：「誠然，壯士啊！心念變幻而難以掌控，但，昆蒂之子啊！藉由修行與捨棄，是可以做到的。

36.「人如果不知如何克制自己，就不可能證得自我了悟；然而對藉由適當方法而努力學會自制的人而言，證得了悟是有可能的。」

37. 阿朱納問道：「主啊！倘若無法克制自己，也無法做靈性沉思；雖無法證得圓滿成就，但卻保有信心（道心），這樣的人會怎樣呢？

38.「我的主！如果既無法克制自己，也無法靈修，那他是不是就毫無希望，而將在靈性道路上迷失，有如浮雲般無有依恃呢？

石頭，而你會在那裡找到我。」（多馬福音第 77 節）；《莊子》知北遊篇中，東郭子問莊子道何在？莊子答：「無所不在」，繼而回答在螻蟻、在瓦甓，甚至在屎溺。

31. The sage who realizes the unity of life and who worships Me in all beings, lives in Me, whatever may be his lot.

32. O Arjuna! He is the perfect saint who, taught by the likeness within himself, sees the same Self everywhere, whether the outer form be pleasurable or painful.

Arjuna said:

33. I do not see how I can attain this state of equanimity which you have revealed, owing to the restlessness of my mind.

34. My Lord! Verily, the mind is fickle and turbulent, obstinate and strong, yea extremely difficult as the wind to control.

Lord Shri Krishna replied:

35. Doubtless, O Mighty One! the mind is fickle and exceedingly difficult to restrain, but, O Son of Kunti! with practice and renunciation it can be done.

36. It is not possible to attain Self-Realization if a man does not know how to control himself; but for him who, striving by proper means, learns such control, it is possible.

Arjuna asked:

37. He who fails to control himself, whose mind falls from spiritual contemplation, who attains not perfection but retains his faith, what of him, my Lord?

38. Having failed in both, my Lord! is he without hope, like a riven cloud having no support, lost on the spiritual road?

39.「我的主！請您為我一次就解此疑惑；除您之外，無人有能力做到。」

40. 克里希納答：「我摯愛的孩子啊！不論此世或來世，他都不會招致滅亡。行正道者，不會招致厄運。

41.「居於正義之人的行列，且已行之多年，儘管偏離了靈性道路，之後仍將轉生在純潔、良善且富足的家庭之中。

42.「又或許他會生於智慧的聖者之家，雖然這樣的轉世是很難得的事。

43.「之後他前世的體驗將會復甦，而藉此之助，他將較以往更殷切地努力去達到圓滿。

44.「不知不覺地，他會重回到他過去世的修行路上。所以嘗試去了悟靈性意識的人，絕對是優於那些只是談論它的人。

45.「靈性修持的人在殷切努力下，如此經歷許多世，罪業消解，終將證得圓滿，達至無上（上帝）。

46.「智者（瑜伽修行者）勝於苦行者，也勝於學者與行動者，因此阿朱納啊！當一位智者（瑜伽修行者）吧。

47.「在我眼中，信心（道心）滿滿，崇拜我，而且也住在我裡面的，這樣的人是神秘者之最。」

39. My Lord! You are worthy to solve this doubt once for all; besides Yourself, there is no one competent to do so.

Lord Shri Krishna replied:

40. My beloved child! There is no destruction for him, either in this world or in the next. No evil fate awaits him who treads the path of righteousness.

41. Having reached the worlds where the righteous dwell, and having remained there for many years, he who has slipped away from the path of spirituality will be born again in the family of the pure, benevolent and prosperous.

42. Or he may be born in the family of the wise sages; though a birth like this is, indeed, very difficult to obtain.

43. Then the experience acquired in his former life will revive, and with its help he will strive for perfection more eagerly than before.

44. Unconsciously he will return to the practices of his old life; so that he who tries to realize spiritual consciousness is certainly superior to one who only talks of it.

45. Then, after many lives, the student of spirituality who earnestly strives, and whose sins are absolved, attains perfection and reaches the Supreme.

46. The wise man is superior to the ascetic and to the scholar and to the man of action; therefore be a wise man, O Arjuna!

47. I look upon him as the best of mystics who, full of faith, worships Me and abides in Me.

這就是聖靈的科學與自我認識的藝術、奧義書之一的聖典——《薄伽梵歌》中，克里希納與阿朱納王子對話的第六章，名為「靜坐與克己自制：禪定瑜伽」。

Thus, in the Holy Book the Bhagavad Gita, one of the Upanishads, in the Science of the Supreme Spirit, in the Art of Self-Knowledge, in the colloquy between the Divine Lord Shri Krishna and the Prince Arjuna, stands the sixth chapter entitled: Meditation and Self Control: Dhyana Yoga.

知識與體驗
Knowledge and Experience

　　本章的標題是知識與體驗，原分別是指闍那（jnana）與毗闍那（vijnana）；以本章而言，前者是指一般的知識與智慧（見第四章），後者則是由親身體驗、了悟而來的智慧（真知或妙慧）。[1] 又或者闍那可說是關於至上的間接知識，而毗闍那則是親證無上的智慧。如果要做比喻的話，闍那就好像是一道美味菜餚的食譜；光讀著食譜（如果想像力夠好的話）只是徒然讓自己口水滿溢。毗闍那則是真正地品嘗菜餚；如此唾液才能與菜餚充分混合，化為滋養我們生命的養分。

　　在這一章中，克里希納揭示祂是所有一切的源頭——造化來自於祂，而不變的永恆自性也是祂；祂既是世界的創造者，也是世界的毀滅者。因為一切都來自於祂，所以人即便是崇拜低等神祇，只要有信心，仍會有結果，因為這些神祇也都來自於祂。只是這樣的人是無明的，唯有全心全意敬拜上主的人，才可以到達上主的無上居所。

　　克里希納在這一章中，再次讚揚了禪定瑜伽。祂說崇拜我的義人依不同之階段分四類：首先是受苦難者，再來是冀求知識者，然後是渴求真理者，最後是獲得智慧者（7:16）。但是祂接著說：

　　「獲得智慧、無止息地靜坐沉思於我，而且唯獨只奉獻於我的智者，是所有這些人當中最優秀的，因為我是為這些智者所摯愛著，而他們也是我鍾愛的。」（7:17）

1　毗闍那在佛教中另有「識」的意思，例如唯識論中所說的第八識即稱為阿賴耶識（alaya vijnana）。

人唯有受苦，才會想要瞭解為何受苦，然後才會渴望真理、踏上尋找生命的道路，最終才是證得智慧圓滿，回歸永恆天家。耶穌也說：「受苦的人有福了，他已經找到了生命。」（《多馬福音》第58節）

釋迦牟尼佛初轉法輪所闡釋的「四聖諦」，依序是苦、集、滅、道，傳達的也是同樣的真理。第一聖諦——苦諦，是瞭解人生之根本是苦：除生老病死四苦外，還有求不得、愛別離、怨憎會等苦；即使有歡樂，所有的樂也都是無常、非永恆的。

第二聖諦——集諦，所闡釋的是瞭解苦的緣由。簡言之，就是所有的苦是由惑（無明）與業聚集而成的。再進一步深究，則可知是因為有貪、嗔、痴等我執，因而在因果業力下，造下身口意的業。要終止所有的苦痛，其終究的圓滿境界就是寂靜涅槃，也就是第三聖諦——滅諦。而第四聖諦——道諦，則是闡述達到圓滿涅槃的方法，包括八正道、戒定慧三學等等。

只是釋迦牟尼佛從不對徒弟說，是否存在一位具人格、同時也是創造與毀滅這所有一切的上帝。或許釋迦牟尼佛是因為出於慈悲，希望徒弟或求道者可以更著眼於靈性的修持，而不是僅僅以有限的頭腦尋找生命的答案吧！

1. 克里希納道：「聽啊！阿朱納！我現在就告訴你，如何藉由全心奉獻於我的靜坐修持，以及皈依我，而能全然圓滿地認識我。

2. 「我將把這個知識揭示給你，也告訴你如何去實行；你一旦做到，這輩子就不再有什麼是值得去擁有的了。

3. 「努力尋求圓滿成就者，萬千人中鮮有一人；即使在這些能獲得奧秘力量的人中，也僅偶然地才有一人能真正地認識我。

4. 「地、水、火、風、以太（空）、心念、理智與個性，是我顯化的造化八性質。[2]

5. 「這是我的低等性質，但勇士啊！當知我還有一個與此不同的高等性質——維繫著這個宇宙的，正是這個生命。

6. 「它是孕育所有眾生的子宮，因為我既是創造諸世界、也是毀滅諸世界的那一位。

7. 「阿朱納啊！沒有比我更高的了；所有一切猶如串連成線的珍珠一般，皆繫於我。

8. 「阿朱納啊！我是水的動性，日月的光。我是吠陀書中的神聖音節「唵」，以太（空）中的音聲，人的生命力。[3]

----

2 前五者（地、水、火、風、以太）是數論中的五大粗略元素；心念、理智與個性則分別是數論中的心、菩提智與我執。詳見導讀中的說明。

Lord Shri Krishna said:

1. Listen, O Arjuna! And I will tell you how you shall know Me in My Full perfection, practicing meditation with your mind devoted to Me, and having Me for your refuge.

2. I will reveal this knowledge unto you, and how it may be realized; which, once accomplished, there remains nothing else worth having in this life.

3. Among thousands of people, scarcely one strives for perfection, and even among those who gain occult powers, perchance but one knows Me in truth.

4. Earth, water, fire, air, ether, mind, intellect and personality – this is the eightfold division of My Manifested Nature.

5. This is My inferior Nature; but distinct from this, O Valiant One! know that My Superior Nature is the very Life which sustains the universe.

6. It is the womb of all beings; for I am He by whom the worlds were created and shall be dissolved.

7. O Arjuna! There is nothing higher than Me; all is strung upon Me as rows of pearls upon a thread.

8. O Arjuna! I am the Fluidity in water, the Light in the sun and in the moon. I am the mystic syllable Om in the Vedic scriptures, the Sound in ether, the Virility in man.

9.「我是泥土的芳香，火焰的光芒。我是所有眾生的生命能，而且我也是苦行者的苦行。

10.「阿朱納啊！你當知道，我是一切萬有的不朽種子，是智者的智慧、榮耀者的榮光。

11.「對於無有執著與欲望的強者，我是他們的力量。而且阿朱納啊！我是眾生心中對正義的渴望。[4]

12.「不論他們生命的本質是純真、熱情或是無明，他們都是從我而來。他們都是在我之中，但我卻不是在他們裡面。

13.「世人為造化三性所幻化的各種現象所迷惑，不知道我比所有這一切都更高，也不知道我是那永恆不變的。

14.「的確，這顯化於造化三性的神聖幻象（摩耶）是難以超越的。只有完全奉獻於我，而且唯獨奉獻於我的人，才能做得到。

15.「罪人、無明者、為幻象迷眩而失去靈性覺知的惡人，以及追求不道德生活的人——他們都找不到我。

16.「阿朱納啊！崇拜我的義人分屬不同的階段：首先是受苦難者，再來是冀求知識者，然後是渴求真理者，最後是獲得智慧者。

---

3 「唵」的英譯也作 AUM。根據英譯，最後一句「人的生命力」似乎也可譯為「男人的氣概」。

4 希瓦南達與多數譯文將最後一句譯為：「我也是眾生中合乎法性的欲望。」（... in all beings, I am the desire unopposed to Dharma.）

9. I am the Fragrance of earth, the Brilliance of fire. I am the Life Force in all beings, and I am the Austerity of the ascetics.

10. Know, O Arjuna! that I am the eternal Seed of being; I am the Intelligence of the intelligent, the Splendor of the resplendent.

11. I am the Strength of the strong, of them who are free from attachment and desire; and, O Arjuna! I am the Desire for righteousness.

12. Whatever be the nature of their life, whether it be Pure or Passionate or Ignorant, they all are derived from Me. They are in Me, but I am not in them.

13. The inhabitants of this world, misled by those natures which the Qualities have engendered, know not that I am higher than them all, and that I do not change.

14. Verily, this Divine Illusion of Phenomena manifesting itself in the Qualities is difficult to surmount. Only they who devote themselves to Me and to Me alone can accomplish it.

15. The sinner, the ignorant, the vile, deprived of spiritual perception by the glamour of Illusion, and he who pursues a godless life – none of them shall find Me.

16. O Arjuna! The righteous who worship Me are grouped by stages: first they who suffer, next they who desire knowledge, then they who thirst after truth, and lastly they who attain wisdom.

17.「獲得智慧、無止息地靜坐沉思於我，而且唯獨只奉獻於我的智者，是所有這些人當中最優秀的，因為我是為這些智者所摯愛著，而他們也是我鍾愛的。

18.「儘管這些義人都有高貴的心，但唯有智者，我把他們視為我的大我；因為智者總是與我共處於平安之境，將我做為他們的最終目標。

19.「經過許多世，智者終將能以如我所是的去了悟我。能夠無處不見上帝，如此開悟之人的確是非常難得。

20.「被種種欲望蒙蔽智慧的人，崇拜低等神祇，依其性情的不同，奉行各種不同的儀式。

21.「但儘管敬拜形式各異，只要供奉者有信心，那麼因著信心這些敬拜也都會有我的保證。

22.「假若他以真信心，行某一形式的崇拜，那麼他也僅只能藉此而滿足其欲望；因為這是我所賦予認可的。

23.「眼光短淺，則其所享有的果實必然也是有限的。崇敬低等神祇者只能到達低等神祇的境界，但崇拜我的人則會來到我這裡。

24.「無明者以為我——無顯化的聖靈——是真的具有人類形象。他們不瞭解我的無上本質是永不變異，而且是至善的。

17. Of all these, he who has gained wisdom, who meditates on Me without ceasing, devoting himself only to Me, he is the best; for by the wise man I am exceedingly beloved and the wise man, too, is beloved by Me.

18. Noble-minded are they all, but the wise man I hold as my own Self; for he, remaining always at peace with Me, makes Me his final goal.

19. After many lives, at last the wise man realizes Me as I am. A man so enlightened that he sees God everywhere is very difficult to find.

20. They in whom wisdom is obscured by one desire or the other, worship the lesser Powers, practicing many rites which vary according to their temperaments.

21. But whatever the form of worship, if the devotee have faith, then upon his faith in that worship do I set My own seal.

22. If he worships one form alone with real faith, then shall his desires be fulfilled through that only; for thus have I ordained.

23. The fruit that comes to men of limited insight is, after all, finite. They who worship the Lower Powers attain them; but those who worship Me come unto Me alone.

24. The ignorant think of Me, who am the Unmanifested Spirit, as if I were really in human form. They do not understand that My Supreme Nature is changeless and most excellent.

25.「並不是所有的人都看得見我，因為我是被塵世的幻象所籠罩著。迷惑的世人不知我是不生不滅的。

26.「阿朱納啊！我知曉過去、現在、未來一切的眾生；但他們並不認識我。

27.「英勇的阿朱納啊！人們活在迷幻的世界中，被衝突對立的感官炫麗所欺瞞，因好惡的情感而迷惘。

28.「但對於行事正直的人而言，他們的罪業業已消解，不被衝突對立的情緒所迷惑，他們以堅定的決心敬拜我。

29.「皈依我，致力於從生老病死循環中解脫的人，他們了悟無上聖靈——也就是他們自己的真正自性——而於其自性中，所有作為皆自得圓滿。

30.「凡能於世間生命中以及一切獻祭中看到我，以純淨神性見我，其內心穩定，他們住在我之內，即使是在臨命終時，亦復如是。」[5]

這就是聖靈的科學與自我認識的藝術、奧義書之一的聖典——《薄伽梵歌》中，克里希納與阿朱納王子對話的第七章，名為「知識與體驗」。

---

5 多數譯文與普羅希的譯文不同。以希瓦南達為例，其譯文為：「在所有元素中、諸神中，以及獻祭中，看到我的人，在其臨命終時，亦安住於我。」（Those who know Me with the Adhibhuta [pertaining to the elements], the Adhidaiva [pertaining to the gods], and Adhiyajna [pertaining to the sacrifice], know Me even at the time of death, steadfast in mind.）

25. I am not visible to all, for I am enveloped by the illusion of Phenomena. This deluded world does not know Me as the Unborn and the Imperishable.

26. I know, O Arjuna! all beings in the past, the present and the future; but they do not know Me.

27. O brave Arjuna! Man lives in a fairy world, deceived by the glamour of opposite sensations, infatuated by desire and aversion.

28. But those who act righteously, in whom sin has been destroyed, who are free from the infatuation of the conflicting emotions, they worship Me with firm resolution.

29. Those who make Me their refuge, who strive for liberation from decay and death, they realize the Supreme Spirit, which is their own real Self, and in which all action finds its consummation.

30. Those who see Me in the life of the world, in the universal sacrifice, and as pure Divinity, keeping their minds steady, they live in Me, even in the crucial hour of death.

Thus, in the Holy Book the Bhagavad Gita, one of the Upanishads, in the Science of the Supreme Spirit, in the Art of Self-Knowledge, in the Colloquy between the Divine Lord Shri Krishna and the Prince Arjuna, stand the seventh chapter, entitled: Knowledge and Experience.

8

無上聖靈

The Supreme Spirit

在這一章中，克里希納談論到兩個主題：一是世界的生滅，另一是生命的輪迴。關於第一個主題，克里希納說這個世界有生有滅，循環不已，眾生亦然；這與佛經所說的成住壞空、輪迴循環一般無二。

關於第二個主題，克里希納的話或許可以看成是印度教版本的《阿彌陀經》。祂說我們在臨命終時，心不論繫念在哪個世界，就會去到那裡（8:6）。因此，只要在臨終時唯獨想著上主，而且就以這樣的念頭離開肉身，我們就會到達上主的無上住所（8:5）。

釋迦牟尼佛在《阿彌陀經》中也說：

「舍利弗。若有善男子善女人，聞說阿彌陀佛，執持名號，若一日、若二日，若三日，若四日，若五日，若六日，若七日，一心不亂，其人臨命終時，阿彌陀佛，與諸聖眾，現在其前。是人終時，心不顛倒，即得往生阿彌陀佛極樂國土。」

佛教淨土宗所修持的，就是以頌持阿彌陀佛為主的唸佛法門。

如果真要比較，或許我們可說西方極樂世界仍是有形有象的世界（或許是受限於文字的有限使然？），而即便往生極樂世界，可能離開悟、成佛還很遠，只是少了我們這五濁惡世的諸多考驗，比較不會再造業、沉淪（淨土法門強調的要點之一就是「帶業往生」）。相較之下，克里希納所允諾的，是到達那永恆不滅的「未顯現」——上主的無上居所（8:20）。只是同樣

的，這並不是一蹴可及的，而是有賴於持之以恆的修持與堅定的信念（8:6-8:10）。

1. 阿朱納問道：「萬主之主啊！人們稱之為無上聖靈（梵）的，究竟是什麼？什麼是人的靈性本質？什麼是律則？又何謂物質，何謂神性？

2. 「統轄人們心中獻祭精神的，究竟是誰？那些已習得克己自制者，於臨命終時，如何能認識您呢？」

3. 克里希納答道：「無上聖靈（梵）是至高、不滅的自性，祂的本質就是靈性意識。諸世界是由聖靈的顯化所創造與維繫著的，這個顯化即稱為律則。

4. 「物質是由各種無常的形象所構成的。神性就是無上自性。你族中最尊貴的人啊！啟發人們心中獻祭精神的，正是我本人，而今以人類的形象站在你面前。

5. 「不論何人，只要在臨終時唯獨想念著我，而且就以這樣的念頭離開肉身、繼續前行，這樣的人必然會認識我。

6. 「臨命終時，心不論繫念在哪個世界，那裡就會是他的去處。

7. 「因此時時靜坐冥思於我，並且戰鬥；只要心念與理智都堅定專注於我，你就確然會來到我這裡。

8. 「心不逸散、恆常靜坐冥思者，臻於無上聖靈之境。

Arjuna asked:

1. O Lord of Lords! What is that which is called the Supreme Spirit, what is man's Spiritual Nature, and what is the Law? What is Matter and what is Divinity?

2. Who is it who rules the spirit of sacrifice in man; and at the time of death how may those who have learned self-control come to the knowledge of You?

The Lord Shri Krishna replied:

3. The Supreme Spirit is the Highest Imperishable Self, and Its Nature is spiritual consciousness. The worlds have been created and are supported by an emanation from the Spirit which is called the Law.

4. Matter consists of the forms that perish; Divinity is the Supreme Self; and He who inspires the spirit of sacrifice in man, O noblest of your race! is I myself, Who now stand in human form before thee.

5. Whosoever at the time of death thinks only of Me, and thinking thus leaves the body and goes forth, assuredly he will know Me.

6. On whatever sphere of being the mind of a man may be intent at the time of death, thither will he go.

7. Therefore meditate always on Me, and fight; if your mind and your reason be fixed on Me, to Me shall you surely come.

8. He whose mind does not wander, and who is engaged in constant meditation, attains the Supreme Spirit.

9.「但凡靜坐冥思於那無所不在、古老、既小於原子卻又是所有一切的統領者與維繫者、不可思議、閃耀如日且超越黑暗之所能及的上主；

10.「離開肉身時,能心念堅定不移並充滿虔敬,藉由靜坐冥想於兩眉之間所聚集的所有生命能的力量,此人將證得無上。

11.「現在我將簡要地解說經典中所宣說的不朽的目標,這個目標是當神秘主義者(靈修者)從熱情中解脫時所證得的境界,也正是為了這個目標,讓他們安於遵守其禁慾的誓言。

12.「關閉身體的孔竅,將意念的力量拉回到心中,並藉由靜坐冥想的力量,將其生命能凝聚於腦部;

13.「複誦那象徵永恆的音節「唵」,總是繫念著我,如此當他離開肉身、繼續前行時,就會達至無上聖靈之境。

14.「時時想著我,此外別無所思,對於這麼有信心的信徒而言,阿朱納啊!我是有求必應的。

15.「如此來到我這裡的偉大靈魂,無須再經歷俗世生活的悲慘與死亡,因為他們已獲得圓滿成就。

16.「十方世界,包括整個造化,來來去去,有成有壞;但阿朱納啊!凡來到我這裡的人,就不再有轉世輪迴。

9. Whoso meditates on the Omniscient, the Ancient, more minute than the atom, yet the Ruler and Upholder of all, Unimaginable, Brilliant like the Sun, beyond the reach of darkness;

10. He who leaves the body with mind unmoved and filled with devotion, by the power of his meditation gathering between his eyebrows his whole vital energy, attains the Supreme.

11. Now I will speak briefly of the imperishable goal, proclaimed by those versed in the scriptures, which the mystic attains when free from passion, and for which he is content to undergo the vow of continence.

12. Closing the gates of the body, drawing the forces of his mind into the heart and by the power of meditation concentrating his vital energy in the brain;

13. Repeating OM, the Symbol of Eternity, holding Me always in remembrance, he who thus leaves his body and goes forth reaches the Spirit Supreme.

14. To him who thinks constantly of Me and of nothing else, to such an ever-faithful devotee, O Arjuna! am I ever accessible.

15. Coming thus unto Me, these great souls go no more to the misery and death of earthly life, for they have gained perfection.

16. The worlds, with the whole realm of creation, come and go; but, O Arjuna! whoso comes to Me, for him there is nor rebirth.

17.「了知寰宇之日與夜者，知道創世的一個白天是一千個循環（週期），而創世的一個夜晚也是同樣長的時間。[1]

18.「當白日來臨時，萬物自『未顯現』中陸續顯化，而當黑夜降臨時，又復歸於『未顯現』之中。[2]

19.「當宇宙的夜晚降臨，一再於此世界輪迴的同一群眾生，將會消失湮滅，然後於破曉時刻再重新出現。這是注定如此的。

20.「因此真相是，存在一『永恆的未顯現』，是超越於『未顯現的創世聖靈』之上的，而即使所有眾生毀滅，祂也依然永存不滅。[3]

21.「智者說那未顯現且不滅的，是最高的目標；而一旦達成，就不用再來。那正是我的神聖居所。

----

1 這裡的白天與夜晚可視為一個世界的創生與毀壞。印度教思想中，宇宙的（最小）週期從正法的黃金時代，到末法時代（Kali Yuga），歷經四個時期，共 432 萬年，合稱一「摩奴生」（manvantara）。一千個摩奴生構成梵神（Brahma）的一個白天，之後則是同樣時間長度的梵神之夜晚。如此一個白晝和一個黑夜形成一劫（kalpa）（見 Shattuck；1999，第 61 頁）。

2 商羯羅的「二梵說」將「梵」的表現分為「上梵」（也稱無形之梵或無相梵；Nirguna-Brahman）與「下梵」（也稱有形之梵或有相梵；Saguna-Brahman），前者是絕對的真理，後者則是相對的存在。概念上，前者是宇宙的本體，它是萬物生起、存續和歸滅的根本；是絕對者，純粹精神的。後者是萬有的本源，創造此現象世界（見孫晶；2007 與 Shattuck；1999）。大致而言，前者相當於菩盧薩，而後者則是造化；嚴格一點說，則菩盧薩包含二者。這裡的「未顯現」當指下梵。

3 這裡克里希納指出「未顯現」有兩類：一是「未顯現的創世聖靈」（意指創造、毀滅此世界的聖靈，同樣也是「未顯現」），也就是前註中所說的「下梵」；另一是「永恆的未顯現」，即前註中所說的「上梵」。

----

17. Those who understand the cosmic day and cosmic night know that one day of creation is a thousand cycles, and that the night is of equal length.

18. At the dawning of that day all objects in manifestation stream forth from the Unmanifest, and when evening falls they are dissolved into It again.

19. The same multitude of beings, which have lived on earth so often, all are dissolved as the night of the universe approaches, to issue forth anew when morning breaks. Thus is it ordained.

20. In truth, therefore, there is the Eternal Unmanifest, which is beyond and above the Unmanifest Spirit of Creation, which is never destroyed when all these beings perish.

21. The wise say that the Unmanifest and Indestructible is the highest goal of all; when once that is reached, there is no return. That is My Blessed Home.

22.「阿朱納啊！那最高的上帝，既是遍及宇宙，且又是所有
眾生的居所，是只有全心奉獻的人才能達到的。

23.「阿朱納啊！我現在要告訴你，當神秘主義者（修行者）
離世時，什麼情況不會回來，什麼情況需再回來。[4]

24.「如果認識無上聖靈（梵）的聖哲在夏至來臨前的六個月、
在月亮漸圓的那半個月、在白晝、於火與光明中離世，那
麼他會達至無上。

25.「但如果是在冬至來臨之前的六個月、在月亮漸虧的那半
個月、在夜晚、於昏暗中離世，那麼他只能到達月光，且
需再轉世。[5]

26.「這兩條離開世界的光明與黑暗道路一直都是並存的。踏
上前者，就不需回來；選擇後者，則需回來。

27.「阿朱納啊！了知這些道路的聖者無有迷惑。因此終生不
斷地靜坐冥想吧。

28.「了知此奧秘的聖哲，其功德超越研讀經典、獻祭、苦行
與布施所得的功德，而且達到了太初的無上住所。」

4　普羅希註明 23-26 這四句經文有可能是後世篡改加入的：他認為這幾句與文中的其他內
容不相符，因為這幾句經文是以隱喻的方式呈現，再則是這意味著「俗世」現象是由「靈
性」決定的。普羅希認為這幾句有可能不是原經文的內容，而是後人為了某些原因（例
如鑑別修行者的靈性程度）而加入的。譯者認為這樣的說法不無可能；這幾句經文敘述
的似乎是內在的境界，而不是外在的物質世界。

5　這裡似乎隱含著「修行者仍在三界內，因此需要再輪迴轉世」之意。

22. O Arjuna! That Highest God, in whom all beings abide, and who pervades the entire universe, is reached only by whole-hearted devotion.

23. Now I will tell you, O Arjuna! of the times at which, if the mystics go forth, they do not return, and at which they go forth only to return.

24. If, knowing the Supreme Spirit, the sage goes forth with fire and light, in the daytime, in the fortnight of the waxing moon, and in the six months before the Northern summer solstice, he will attain the Supreme.

25. But if he departs in gloom, at night, during the fortnight of the waning moon and in the six months before the Southern solstice, then he reaches but lunar light, and he will be born again.

26. These bright and dark paths out of the world have always existed. Whoso takes the former, returns not; he who chooses the latter, returns.

27. O Arjuna! The saint knowing these paths is not confused. Therefore meditate perpetually.

28. The sage who knows this passes beyond all merit that comes from the study of the scriptures, from sacrifice, from austerities and charity, and reaches the Supreme Primeval Abode.

這就是聖靈的科學與自我認識的藝術、奧義書之一的聖典——《薄伽梵歌》中，克里希納與阿朱納王子對話的第八章，名為「無上聖靈」。

Thus, in the Holy Book the Bhagavad Gita, one of the Upanishads, in the Science of the Supreme Spirit, in the Art of Self-Knowledge, in the Colloquy between the Divine Lord Shri Krishna and the Prince Arjuna, stand the eight chapter, entitled: The Supreme Spirit.

- Chapter -

9

....

科學之最與奧秘之最

The Science of Sciences and the
Mystery of Mysteries

　　在這一章中，克里希納再次揭示祂是一切的源頭，也是所有一切。因此人們不論心中祈求什麼，也都會有祂的允諾。所以人即使行善布施，也讀經祭祀，但如果這些背後的驅使力量是私欲，那麼其回報也就只是人天福報。即使是往生後得享天堂榮耀，一旦福報用盡，仍須一再經歷生死輪迴。

　　為此，克里希納揭示了有名的兩句詩文（9:27-9:28）：

　　「不論做什麼、吃什麼，獻祭或布施什麼，或者修何苦行，都把它們作為對我的供養。」

　　「如此你的行為就不會伴隨著結果，不論是好的或不好的；藉著捨棄的心，你將會來到我這裡，並獲得自在解脫。」

　　一些版本的 9:27 節有點不同。例如，伊斯瓦蘭的譯文是這樣的：

　　「不論做什麼——飲食、獻祭、布施，甚至是所受的苦，或者修何苦行，都把它們作為對我的供養。」

　　許多宗教都強調供養的重要性，但「無我」布施才是供養的真諦。例如，佛教常常強調供養三寶（佛、法、僧）的功德利益，但《金剛經》指出，唯有無執著的布施、供養，方能有不可思量的功德。相對地，如果是存著利益自己的心而行供養，那麼就只能獲得有限的福報；此間之差別不可不慎。

　　佛經中一個很有名的例子，是關於白淨比丘尼的故事。釋

迦牟尼佛在世時，有一位生於富裕家庭的女徒弟，在出生時就神奇地被白紗裹身，所以她的父母將她命名為「白淨」。長大後的白淨端莊出眾，很多人都想娶她為妻。但她一心只想修行解脫，她的父母也是佛陀虔誠的信徒，就帶她去見佛陀，請求讓她出家為尼。佛陀答應了白淨的祈求，而白淨身上的白衣也自動變成了袈裟。修行不久，白淨比丘尼就證得了阿羅漢果。

弟子們很驚訝於白淨比丘尼何以有如此殊勝的因緣，於是佛陀為弟子們解釋原委。原來在久遠以前，白淨原是一位很貧窮的女子，與丈夫唯有的財產就是一件破舊毯子，所以兩人只能輪流出門乞食。一天她遇到一位比丘，比丘告訴她布施供養三寶有很大功德，可脫離貧苦，因此她就跟丈夫商量把唯一的財產供養給當時的在世佛。

這個誠心供養的結果就是在往後的九十一劫，她每一世出生之時，都有白紗裹身，並且生生世世衣食豐裕無缺。很多人因此而讚嘆供養的福報不可思議。但也正由於白淨的初心只是為了脫離貧苦，因此竟然要經歷了九十一劫（數億萬年）才遇到釋迦牟尼佛，然後才能得修行解脫。由此可見供養的初發心的重要。

我們一般心目中的供養，當然是認為自己擁有的有價值的東西，才拿來做供養。但是真正對上帝的供養，是將所有一切，不論是好的或不好的，包括苦難，都獻給上帝——這才是供養的真正意義。因為所有一切的身口意都是對上主的供養，因此就是無我，也就無有「業障」；因著對上主絕對的信心，加上不執著的捨棄之心，主也允諾我們必然能夠與祂合而為

一。這就是本章所說的科學與奧秘之最。

　　這裡，科學一詞是廣義的。根據維基百科的定義，科學原先只對應於自然領域的知識，後經擴充而應用在社會、思維等領域，如社會學。它涵蓋兩方面含意：一是致力於揭示自然真相，而對自然作理由充分的觀察或研究；二是通過這樣的研究而獲得有組織體系的知識。因此，靈性知識的探究也是一項科學，事實上是最根本的科學。

1. 克里希納道：「既然你已不再疑惑，我現在將為你揭示最深邃的奧秘；當你親身經驗，將可讓你解脫，免於罪業。

2. 「這是最原先的科學，至高無上的秘密，最純淨且最好的；合乎直觀又合於法性；修持它而得到的喜樂不可思量。

3. 「對此教理沒有信心者尋不著我，只會於此無常世界失落浮沉。

4. 「我遍及整個世界，但我的形象是不可見的。所有生物的生命本質（存有）都在我內，然而我並不為其所限。

5. 「儘管如是，他們並無意識到是住在我內。雖然我 —— 無上自性 —— 是一切萬有的因與維繫者，但我仍在這一切之外 —— 這就是我的神聖權柄。

6. 「猶如強風，雖吹向四方，但除了虛空，它別無休憩之處；所有眾生亦然：除我之外，他們別無歸處。

7. 「阿朱納啊！每個宇宙循環週期結束時，所有眾生都會回歸到造化的國度之中，也就是我的一部分；而在下一個週期之始，我會把他們再度送出。

8. 「藉造化之助，我一再將所有眾生送出 —— 不論他們是否願意，因為他們都是由我的旨意統轄的。

Lord Shri Krishna said:

1. I will now reveal to you, since you doubt not, that profound mysticism, which when followed by experience, shall liberate you from sin.

2. This is the Premier Science, the Sovereign Secret, the Purest and Best; intuitional, righteous; and to him who practices it pleasant beyond measure.

3. They who have no faith in this teaching cannot find Me, but remain lost in the purlieus of this perishable world.

4. The whole world is pervaded by Me, yet my form is not seen. All living things have their being in Me, yet I am not limited by them.

5. Nevertheless, they do not consciously abide in Me. Such is My Divine Sovereignty that though I, the Supreme Self, am the cause and upholder of all, yet I remain outside.

6. As the mighty wind, though moving everywhere, has no resting place but space, so have all these beings no home but Me.

7. All beings, O Arjuna! return at the close of every cosmic cycle into the realm of Nature, which is a part of Me, and at the beginning of the next I send them forth again.

8. With the help of Nature, again and again I pour forth the whole multitude of beings, whether they will or no, for they are ruled by My Will.

9.「但我的這些行動並不會束縛我。我仍然在外，無有執著。

10.「在我引領之下，造化創造出所有會動與不會動的事物。阿朱納啊！宇宙就是如此周行而不殆。

11.「愚者輕忽我，以人類形象看待我。他們不知道在我的較高本性裡，我是上主——是一切萬有的上帝。

12.「他們的希望、作為與知識，盡皆枉然無益；他們既無見識，且又虛假、粗野與邪惡。

13.「但阿朱納啊！那些聖靈充滿的偉大靈魂，他們敬拜我，心中唯獨只繫念著我，因為他們知道我是存有的不朽源頭。

14.「他們總是讚美我，奮力堅守誓言，向我頂禮跪拜，他們以專注奉獻的心，不間斷地禮拜我。

15.「另有一些人以我是『一』、是『多』，是無所不在、遍及一切，他們全然覺知地如是敬拜我。

16.「我是祭品、獻祭與禮拜；我是燃油與讚歌，我是供奉給火的油膏，我是火本身，我就是供養的行為。

17.「我是宇宙的父親與母親；我既是宇宙的養育者，也是它的祖父；我是可知曉的與純真的；我是『唵』；我是聖典。

9. But these acts of Mine do not bind Me. I remain outside and unattached.

10. Under my guidance, Nature produces all things movable and immovable. Thus it is, O Arjuna! that this universe revolves.

11. Fools disregard Me, seeing Me clad in human form. They know not that in My higher nature I am the Lord God of all.

12. Their hopes are vain, their actions worthless, their knowledge futile; they are without sense, deceitful, barbarous and godless.

13. But the Great Souls, O Arjuna! filled with My Divine Spirit, they worship Me, they fix their minds on Me and on Me alone, for they know that I am the imperishable Source of being.

14. Always extolling Me, strenuous, firm in their vows, prostrating themselves before Me, they worship Me continually with concentrated devotion.

15. Others worship Me with full consciousness as the One, the Manifold, the Omnipresent, the Universal.

16. I am the Oblation, the Sacrifice and the Worship; I am the Fuel and the Chant, I am the Butter offered to the fire, I am the Fire itself; and I am the Act of offering.

17. I am the Father of the universe and its Mother; I am its Nourisher and its Grandfather; I am the Knowable and the Pure; I am Oм; and I am the Sacred Scriptures.

18.「我是目標、維護者、上主、見證人、家園、庇護所,是愛人,是源頭;我是生與死;我是不朽的泉源與種子。

19.「我是太陽的熱,我釋出與留住雨水。我是死亡與永生;我是存有與非存有。

20.「有些人頌讀經典,飲用神奇的蘇摩汁而淨化罪業,但卻以牲品禮拜我,祈禱我會帶領他們安抵天堂;他們會抵達掌管造化諸神者所居住的神聖世界,並享有天堂樂園的饗宴。[1]

21.「然而儘管他們享有天堂樂園的輝煌榮耀,但是一旦福報享盡,他們就會再降生於這有生死的娑婆世界。他們雖遵循經文,但因為他們追尋的僅是個人欲望的滿足,所以他們必須一再地來回轉世。

22.「但人如果靜坐冥想於我,且唯獨我,並且能不論身處何地,時時刻刻敬拜我,我會以我自己來實現他心中的渴望,並且確保他所證得的任何境界。

23.「即使是那些敬拜低等神祇的人,只要他們是以信心禮拜,如是他們也是在禮拜我,雖然方式並不正確。

---

1 根據維基百科,蘇摩果汁是印度婆羅門教儀式中飲用的一種飲料,得自於某種至今未知的植物(或真菌)的汁液。有些中文翻譯為「甘露」或「甘露水」,據說在甚深禪定中,眉心輪(也稱第三眼,大約位置在松果體附近)會泌出甘露,讓人產生一種開悟的狂喜。

18. I am the Goal, the Sustainer, the Lord, the Witness, the Home, the Shelter, the Lover and the Origin; I am Life and Death; I am the Fountain and the Seed Imperishable.

19. I am the Heat of the Sun, I release and hold back the Rains. I am Death and Immortality; I am Being and Not-Being.

20. Those who are versed in the scriptures, who drink the mystic Soma-juice and are purified from sin, but who while worshipping Me with sacrifices, pray that I will lead them to heaven – they reach the holy world where lives the Controller of the Powers of Nature, and they enjoy the feasts of Paradise.

21. Yet although they enjoy the spacious glories of Paradise, nevertheless, when their merit is exhausted, they are born again into this world of mortals. They have followed the letter of the scriptures, yet because they have sought but to fulfill their own desires, they must depart and return again and again.

22. But if a man will meditate on Me and Me alone, and will worship Me always and everywhere, I will take upon Myself the fulfillment of his aspiration, and I will safeguard whatsoever he shall attain.

23. Even those who worship the lesser Powers, if they do so with faith, they thereby worship Me, though not in the right way.

24.「我是獻祭的衷心接受者，而且我是獻祭的真正主人（上主）。但這些供養者並不是真正地認識我，所以他們還會再墜落回來。

25.「低等神祇的信眾歸於低等神祇，祖靈的敬拜者歸於祖靈；崇拜黑暗邪靈者也必將走向邪靈；因此同樣地，敬拜我的人會來到我這裡。

26.「不論人供養我什麼，但凡一葉、一花、一果，或水，我都接受，因為那是以虔敬與純淨的心供養的。

27.「不論做什麼、吃什麼，獻祭或布施什麼，或者修何苦行，都把它們作為對我的供養。

28.「如此你的行為就不會伴隨著結果，不論是好的或不好的；藉著捨棄的心，你將會來到我這裡，並獲得自在解脫。

29.「我對所有眾生都是相同的，既不偏愛也無厭惡。然誠心敬拜我者，他們住在我內，而我也住在他們之內。

30.「即使是罪業深重者，如果全心敬拜我，也會被視為義人，因為他已踏上正途。

31.「不久他就會證得靈性，而永恆的平安將是屬於他的。阿朱納啊！相信我，我的信徒永不失落。

32.「因為即使是罪人之子、人們誤稱為柔弱的性別（女人）、商賈或是工人，只要皈依我，他們就能證得至上。

24. I am the willing recipient of sacrifice, and I am its true Lord. But these do not know Me in truth, and so they sink back.

25. The votaries of the lesser Powers go to them; the devotees of spirits go to them; they who worship the Powers of Darkness, to such Powers shall they go; and so, too, those who worship Me shall come unto Me.

26. Whatever someone offers to Me, whether it be a leaf, or a flower, or fruit, or water, I accept it, for it is offered with devotion and purity of mind.

27. Whatever you do, whatever you eat, whatever you sacrifice and give, whatever austerities you practice, do all as an offering to Me.

28. So shall your action be attended by no result, either good or bad; but through the spirit of renunciation you shall come to Me and be free.

29. I am the same to all beings. I favor none, and I hate none. But those who worship Me devotedly, they live in Me, and I in them.

30. Even the most sinful, if he worships Me with his whole heart, shall be considered righteous, for he is treading the right path.

31. He shall attain spirituality ere long, and Eternal Peace shall be his. O Arjuna! Believe Me, My devotee is never lost.

32. For even the children of sinful parents, and those miscalled the weaker sex, and merchants, and laborers, if only they will make Me their refuge, they shall attain the Highest.

33.「更何況是上帝神聖的使者、信徒,以及聖潔的統治者
　　呢?因此,既已生於此無常的悲慘世界,你就也應敬拜
　　我。

34.「將心念繫於我,把你自己奉獻給我,為我犧牲,臣服於
　　我,以我為你渴望的對象,那麼你就必然會與我——也就
　　是你的自性——合而為一。」

這就是聖靈的科學與自我認識的藝術、奧義書之一的聖
典——《薄伽梵歌》中,克里希納與阿朱納王子對話的第九
章,名為「科學之最與奧秘之最」。

33. What need then to mention the holy ministers of God, the devotees and the saintly rulers? You, therefore, born in this changing and miserable world, should worship Me too.

34. Fix your mind on Me, devote yourself to Me, sacrifice for Me, surrender to Me, make Me the object of your aspirations, and too shall assuredly become one with Me, Who am your own Self.

Thus, in the Holy Book the Bhagavad Gita, one of the Upanishads, in the Science of the Supreme Spirit, in the Art of Self-Knowledge, in the colloquy between the Divine Lord Shri Krishna and the Prince Arjuna, stands the ninth chapter, entitled: The Science of Sciences and the Mystery of Mysteries.

10

神聖顯化

The Divine Manifestations

在這一章中，克里希納更進一步地向阿朱納揭示所有一切都來自於祂；這不僅僅是包含有形與無形的宇宙與眾生，也包含所有不具實質的語言、概念等。事實上，所有一切原本就是上主的概念；我們的眼耳鼻舌身意、所有的意識都是概念。有句話說：「人因概念而生，因概念而死，因概念而了生脫死。」其意義也就在此。

克里希納在這一章中，以「正面表列」的方式，向阿朱納揭示了祂神聖面向的一小部分。因為其中所提到的人事物頗多與印度的傳統或歷史有關，所以對多數人而言較難有深切的感受。這一章的重點之一，或許是提醒我們應以最高的上主，作為我們靜坐冥思的對象吧！

1. 克里希納道：「王子啊！現在請聽我的無上建言，我是為了你的福祉才告訴你的，因為你是我所摯愛的。

2.「不論是神學導師或是偉大的苦行者，都不知道我從何而來，雖然他們都是從我而來。

3.「知曉我是無生、無始、宇宙之主，這樣的人已去除迷惑，從所有想像得到的罪業中解脫。

4.「聰明、智慧、不惑、寬恕、真實、自制、寧靜、苦、樂、生、死、畏與無畏；

5.「不傷害（非暴力）、泰然平等、滿足、苦行、布施、名譽與失敗，所有種種眾生的特質，全都是從我而來。[1]

6.「七大先知、人類的始祖——古老的四位，以及法典設立者，皆自我的旨意而誕生、直接從我而來。人類是自他們繁衍而來的。[2]

7.「能夠正確瞭解我顯化的榮光，以及我的創造大能的人，毫無疑問地會證得圓滿平安。

8.「我是一切萬有的源頭，萬物皆由我流出。因此，智者以堅定不移的誠心敬拜我。

----

1 不傷害（ahimsa），也就是非暴力（non-violence），是印度教、佛教與耆那教相當重要的戒律（或者說是行事原則）。

2 七大先知分別為 Mareechi、Atri、Angira、Pulah、Kratu、Pulastya、Vahishta（普羅希原註）。四位人類的始祖則是 Sanak、Sanandan、Sanatan 與 Sanatkumar；這四位是梵天神（lord Brahma）的兒子，人類自他們四位而來。

Lord Shri Krishna said:

1. Now, O Prince! Listen to My supreme advice, which I give you for the sake of your welfare, for you are My beloved.

2. Neither the professors of divinity nor the great ascetics know my origin, for I am the source of them all.

3. He who knows Me as the unborn, without beginning, the Lord of the universe, he, stripped of his delusions, becomes free from all conceivable sin.

4. Intelligence, wisdom, non-illusion, forgiveness, truth, self-control, calmness, pleasure, pain, birth, death, fear and fearlessness;

5. Harmlessness, equanimity, contentment, austerity, beneficence, fame and failure, all these, the characteristics of beings, spring from Me only.

6. The seven Great Seers, the Progenitors of mankind, the Ancient Four, and the Lawgivers were born of My will and came forth direct from Me. The race of humankind has sprung from them.

7. He who rightly understands My manifested glory and My Creative Power, beyond doubt attains perfect Peace.

8. I am the source of all; from Me everything flows. Therefore the wise worship Me with unchanging devotion.

9.「他們心念專注在我，生命融入於我，並且彼此相互啟迪，總是感到滿足與喜悅。

10.「總是以虔誠與愛心敬拜我的人，我賜予他們明辨的能力，來引導他們到我這裡。

11.「藉著我的恩典，我活在他們的心中；而且我以智慧之光芒將其無明之黑暗驅離。」

12. 阿朱納問：「您是無上聖靈、永恆的家園、神聖中之至聖、永恆的神聖自性（菩盧薩）、太初的上帝、無生與無所不在的。

13.「眾先知與聖哲那瑞達都這麼說，阿西塔、德瓦拉與毗耶娑也如是說；而您自己也這麼說。

14.「主啊！我相信您所告訴我的，因為不論是信神者或不信者，他們都無法瞭解您的顯化。

15.「唯有您認識您自己——以您自性的力量；您是無上聖靈、所有一切眾生的源頭與主宰、眾王之王、宇宙的統治者。

16.「請告訴我所有關於您的榮光顯化，就是藉著這顯化，您遍及一切世界。

9. With minds concentrated on Me, with lives absorbed in Me, and enlightening each other, they ever feel content and happy.

10. To those who are always devout and who worship Me with love, I give the power of discrimination, which leads them to Me.

11. By My grace, I live in their hearts; and I dispel the darkness of ignorance by the shining light of wisdom.

Arjuna asked:

12. You are the Supreme Spirit, the Eternal Home, the Holiest of the Holy, the Eternal Divine Self, the Primal God, the Unborn and the Omnipresent.

13. So have said the seers and the divine sage Narada; as well as Asita, Devala and Vyasa; and You Yourself also say it.

14. I believe in what You have said, my Lord! For neither the godly nor the godless comprehend Your manifestation.

15. You alone know Yourself, by the power of Your Self; you the Supreme Spirit, the Source and Master of all being, the Lord of Lords, the Ruler of the Universe.

16. Please tell me all about Your glorious manifestations, by means of which You pervade the world.

17. 「師父啊！我如何能藉由不斷的靜坐冥思來認識您呢？我的主！可否告訴我您的種種顯化，讓我在靜坐冥思您時能有所憑藉？

18. 「我祈求您，再次告訴我您全然的力量與榮耀；因為我覺得聆聽您不朽的話語，永遠都聽不夠。」

19. 克里希納答：「好吧，我摯愛的朋友。我將為你揭開關於我榮耀的幾個主要面向。若要說起它的全然面貌，那是永無止境的啊。

20. 「阿朱納啊！我是自性，安置於所有眾生的心中；我是啟始、是生命，也是他們所有一切的終尾（盡頭）。

21. 「在所有的造化諸神中，我是造物主；在光體中，我是太陽；在風中，我是旋風；在眾星中，我是月亮。

22. 「在吠陀經文中，我是讚歌；在造化諸神中，我是雷電（雷神因陀羅）；在各種感官中，我是心；而且我是所有生物內在的理智。[3]

23. 「在維生的諸能力中，我是生命；在異教徒與不信神的人中，我是馬蒙（財神）；我是火、土、風、天、日、月，與眾星中的能量；山岳中，我是梅魯山（須彌山）。

---

3 雷神因陀羅就是佛教經典中的帝釋天。

17. O Master! How shall I, by constant meditation, know You? My Lord! What are Your various manifestations through which I am to mediate on You?

18. Tell me again, I pray, about the fullness of Your power and Your glory; for I feel that I am never satisfied when I listen to Your immortal words.

Lord Shri Krishna replied:

19. So be it, My beloved friend! I will unfold to you some of the chief aspects of My glory. Of its full extent there is no end.

20. O Arjuna! I am the Self, seated in the hearts of all beings; I am the beginning and the life, and I am the end of them all.

21. Of all the creative Powers I am the Creator, of luminaries the Sun; the Whirlwind among the winds, and the Moon among planets.

22. Of the Vedas I am the Hymns, I am the Electric Force in the Powers of Nature; of the senses I am the Mind; and I am the Intelligence in all that lives.

23. Among Forces of Vitality I am the Life, I am Mammon to the heathen and the godless; I am the Energy in fire, earth, wind, sky, heaven, sun, moon and planets; and among mountains I am the Mount Meru.

24.「阿朱納啊！要知道在所有的祭師中，我是使徒布里哈斯帕地；在將領中，我是大將軍司堪達；眾水中，我是海洋。

25.「先知中，我是布瑞谷；在話語中，我是『唵』；在獻祭供養中，我是沉默的祈禱者；在所有不可動搖的事物中，我是喜馬拉雅山。

26.「在樹中，我是神聖的無花果樹（菩提樹）；聖潔的先知中，我是那瑞達；在天堂樂手中，我是他們的領隊齊陀拉塔；在聖哲中，我是迦毘羅。[4]

27.「當知在馬匹中，我是聖馬培格瑟斯；在象群中，我是白象；而在人群中，我是統治者。

28.「在武器中，我是雷電；在乳牛中，我是產量豐碩的（如意牛）；在生育中，我是熱情（愛神堪達帕）；在毒蛇群中，我是眼鏡蛇（蛇王瓦蘇其）。

29.「在蛇群中，我是蛇王；在水族中，我是水中主宰（水神瓦汝那）；我是所有的先祖之父；在統治者中，我是死亡（死神雅瑪）。[5]

---

4 這裡的迦毘羅，應是指數論的創立者迦毘羅仙人。有些譯本譯為卡比爾。就譯者僅知的卡比爾（Kabir, 1440-1518），是與古魯那那克（Guru Nanak; 錫克教的第一位祖師）同時代的印度聖人，當然不會是這裡提到的迦毘羅。

5 印度教的死神雅瑪（Yama），後來演變為佛教（尤其是中國佛教）中的閻羅王。

24. Among the priests, know, O Arjuna! that I am the Apostle Brihaspati; of generals I am Skanda, the Commander-in-Chief, and of waters I am the Ocean.

25. Of the great seers I am Bhrigu, of words I am O_M, of offerings I am the silent prayer, among things immovable I am the Himalayas.

26. Of trees I am the sacred fig-tree, of the divine seers Narada, of the heavenly singers I am Chitraratha, their leader, and of sages I am Kapila.

27. Know that among horses I am Pegasus, the heaven-born; among the lordly elephants I am the White One, and I am the Ruler among men.

28. I am the Thunderbolt among weapons; of cows I am the Cow of Plenty, I am Passion in those who procreate, and I am the Cobra among serpents.

29. I am the King Python among snakes, I am the Aqueous Principle among those that live in water, I am the Father of fathers, and among rulers I am Death.

30.「而且在異教徒中，我是信徒普拉達；在時間中，我是永恆的當下；我是野獸中的獅子，禽鳥中的老鷹。

31.「在淨化者中，我是風；在戰士中，我是羅摩王；在魚類中，我是鱷魚；而在眾河中，我是恆河。

32.「我是造化的開頭、中間與終結；在科學中，我是靈性的科學；在辯論者中，我是議論。

33.「字母中我是 A；在複合詞中我是連繫詞；我是永無止盡的時間；而且是無所不在的維護者。⁶

34.「我是吞噬一切的死亡；我是所有當來一切的根源；我是名譽、財富、言語、記憶、理智、恆常與寬恕。

35.「在讚歌中，我是布里哈薩瑪；在格律中我是葛亞萃：月份中我是十二月；而且我是季節中的春季。

36.「我是騙術中的賭博，以及璀璨中的光輝；我是勝利；我是努力；而且我是純真者的潔性。

37.「我是毗濕奴氏族中的師利克里希納；般度家族中的阿朱納；在聖人中我是毗耶娑；而且在聖哲中我是修克拉阿闍黎。⁷

---

6 「字母中我是 A」原是指梵文的第一個字母。

7 師利（Shri, Sri）意為神聖，是印度用來對聖人的尊稱，冠於名字之前；類似基督宗教中的封聖（例如聖約翰）。

30. And I am the devotee Prahlada among the heathen; of Time I am the Eternal Present; I am the Lion among beasts and the Eagle among birds.

31. I am the Wind among the purifiers, the King Rama among warriors; I am the Crocodile among the fishes, and I am the Ganges among the rivers.

32. I am the Beginning, the Middle and the End in creation; among sciences, I am the science of Spirituality; I am the Discussion among disputants.

33. Of letters I am A; I am the copulative in compound words; I am Time inexhaustible; and I am the all-pervading Preserver.

34. I am all-devouring Death; I am the Origin of all that shall happen; I am Fame, Fortune, Speech, Memory, Intellect, Constancy and Forgiveness.

35. Of hymns I am Brihatsama, of meters I am Gayatri, among the months I am Margashirsha (December) , and I am the Spring among seasons.

36. I am the Gambling of the cheat and the Splendor of the splendid; I am Victory; I am Effort; and I am the Purity of the pure.

37. I am Shri Krishna among the Vrishni-clan and Arjuna among the Pandavas; of the saints I am Vyasa, and I am Shukracharya among the sages.

38.「我是統治者的王權、征戰者的謀略、玄秘的沉默、智者的智慧。

39.「阿朱納啊！我是所有眾生的種子。沒有我，所有會動與不會動的生物都無法生存。

40.「阿朱納啊！我神聖生命的面向是無止盡的。如此之說明，也僅僅是皮毛而已。

41.「任何的榮耀、優秀、美與力，當知那都只是來自我璀璨榮光的吉光片羽罷了。

42.「但所有這些細節對你有何用？阿朱納啊！我只用我自己的小小一部分就維繫著這整個宇宙。」

這就是聖靈的科學與自我認識的藝術、奧義書之一的聖典——《薄伽梵歌》中，克里希納與阿朱納王子對話的第十章，名為「神聖顯化」。

38. I am the Scepter of rulers, the Strategy of the conquerors, the Silence of mystery, the Wisdom of the wise.

39. I am the Seed of all being, O Arjuna! No creature moving or unmoving can live without Me.

40. O Arjuna! The aspects of My divine life are endless. I have mentioned but a few by way of illustration.

41. Whatever is glorious, excellent, beautiful and mighty, be assured that it comes from a fragment of My splendor.

42. But what is the use of all these details to you? O Arjuna! I sustain this universe with only a small part of Myself.

Thus, in the Holy Book the Bhagavad Gita, one of the Upanishads, in the Science of the Supreme Spirit, in the Art of Self-Knowledge, in the colloquy between the Divine Lord Shri Krishna and the Prince Arjuna, stands the tenth chapter, entitled: The Divine Manifestations.

11

宇宙景象

The Cosmic Vision

在這一章中，克里希納賜予阿朱納靈視，看到一般人肉眼所看不到的宇宙景象。上主展示給阿朱納的景象，不只是燦爛榮耀的無上形象，其四射之光芒遠遠超過一千個太陽；祂也呈現了祂作為毀滅者的形象，吞噬了雙方陣營的將士。

克里希納賜予的靈性體驗，一方面預示了這些將士的命運，暗示所有一切都是依上主的旨意而運行的；另一方面，這也隱含著時間是造化的幻象，因為所有一切都業已發生完成。剩下的，或許只是去親身體驗而已。

一些人認為這是克里希納賜予阿朱納的恩典，讓他體驗到三摩地（Samadhi，或譯「入定」）。但也有評論者提醒這種靈視的境界並不是了悟或開悟；開悟伴隨著的是與至上的合一、自我感的消失，但阿朱納在此看到宇宙的樣貌後，卻驚駭不已。

但要怎樣才能了悟或開悟呢？在第九章中，克里希納告訴我們應把所有一切做為對上主的供養，如此行為就不會伴隨著結果，因此祂對阿朱納說：「成為我的工具吧！」（11:33）。在本章的最後，祂更進一步說：

「每一行止都是為我而做，以我為最終的目標，唯獨只愛我而不憎恨任何人，我最親愛的孩子啊！只有這樣的人能了悟我！」（11:55）

1. 阿朱納道：「我的主！為了護佑我，您告訴我有關自性的無上秘密，驅散了環繞著我的幻象。

2. 「主啊！您的眼睛猶如蓮花的花瓣！您已為我詳說生命（存有）的源頭與終尾，以及您自己的不朽莊嚴。

3. 「我相信您所宣說的一切。至高的主啊！現在我渴望能一睹您的神聖容顏。

4. 「眾王之王啊！如果您認為可以讓我看到，就請您為我展現您的永恆自性（大我）。」

5. 克里希納答：「看啊！阿朱納啊！且看我千千百百種顏色、形狀與種類各異的天堂形象！

6. 「你看造化諸神：火、地、風、天，日月星辰與諸天堂世界，所有維生與療癒的力量，以及那流動的風。這種種奇觀，我只揭示給你一人。

7. 「阿朱納啊！且看那整個寰宇，不論是會動或不會動的事物，以及任何你想看到的東西；所有一切全部活在我之內，成為一體！

8. 「但因為用肉眼無法看到我，我且賜給你靈視，瞧！現在你可以一窺我王國的璀璨榮耀了。」

Arjuna said:

1. My Lord! Your words concerning the Supreme Secret of Self, given for my blessing, have dispelled the illusions which surrounded me.

2. O Lord! Whose eyes are like the lotus petal! You have described in detail the origin and the dissolution of being, and Your own Eternal Majesty.

3. I believe all as You have declared it. I long now to have a vision of Your Divine Form, O You Most High!

4. If You think that it can be made possible for me to see it, show me, O Lord of Lords! Your own Eternal Self.

Lord Shri Krishna replied:

5. Behold, O Arjuna! my celestial forms, by hundreds and thousands, various in kind, in color and in shape.

6. Behold the Powers of Nature: fire, earth, wind and sky; the sun, the heavens, the moon, the stars; all the forces of vitality and of healing; and the roving winds. See the myriad wonders revealed to none but you.

7. Here, in Me living as one, O Arjuna! behold the whole universe, movable and immovable, and anything else that you would see.

8. Yet since with mortal eyes you cannot see Me, lo! I give you the Divine Sight. See now the glory of My Sovereignty.

9. 山佳亞續言道：王啊！克里希納 —— 全能的智慧王子 —— 在說了這些話後，就把至偉上帝的無上形象展示在阿朱納的面前。

10. 展現眼前的是，有著無數的眼與口，以及不計其數的奧秘形象，並裝飾著閃亮的飾品與發光發熱的天堂武器。

11. 頭戴天堂花冠、穿著閃亮華服、身塗神聖油膏；祂所示現的，是燦爛輝煌的，不可思議、無有極限，且又無所不在。

12. 即便是千個太陽的火焰加起來，也只不過是微弱地反映出上主的四射光芒而已。

13. 就在這靈視中，阿朱納看到宇宙，雖有著各種樣貌，全部融入於「一」——也就是上主——之中。

14. 爾時阿朱納訝然無語、毛髮聳立、頂禮合十，對主說道，

15. 阿朱納道：「全能的上帝啊！在您裡面，我看到造化諸神、世間各種生物、坐於蓮花座上的造物主（梵天）、諸聖哲，以及閃亮的天使們。

16. 「我見到您有無限形象，彷若處處皆是數不清的臉、眼與四肢；分不清哪裡是頭、哪裡是中間、哪裡是尾。宇宙之主啊！您的形象是無所不在的！

Sanjaya continued:

9. Having thus spoken, O King! The Lord Shri Krishna, the Almighty Prince of Wisdom, showed to Arjuna the Supreme Form of the Great God.

10. There were countless eyes and mouths, and mystic forms innumerable, with shining ornaments and flaming celestial weapons.

11. Crowned with heavenly garlands, clothed in shining garments, anointed with divine unctions, He showed Himself as the Resplendent One, Marvelous, Boundless, Omnipresent.

12. Could a thousand suns blaze forth together, it would be but a faint reflection of the radiance of the Lord God.

13. In that vision Arjuna saw the universe, with its manifold shapes, all embraced in One, its Supreme Lord.

14. Thereupon Arjuna, dumb with awe, his hair on end, his head bowed, his hands clasped in salutation, addressed the Lord thus:

Arjuna said:

15. O Almighty God! I see in You the powers of Nature, the various Creatures of the world, the Progenitor on his lotus throne, the Sages and the shining angels.

16. I see You, infinite in form, with, as it were, faces, eyes and limbs everywhere; no beginning, no middle, no end; O Lord of the Universe, whose Form is universal!

17. 「我見到您戴著皇冠，手持權杖與鐵餅（武器）；光芒四射，令我難以直視：您是如此閃耀，猶如熊熊烈火般耀眼，像烈日般燦爛炫目，不可思量。

18. 「您是不朽的，是唯一值得認識的，是宇宙的無價寶庫，是永恆生命的不朽守護，也是永生的聖靈。

19. 「無起始、無中間，亦無盡頭，您的力量無限，您的臂膀含納一切，日月是您的眼睛，您的臉龐散放著獻祭的火焰，光芒遍灑寰宇。

20. 「您自身充滿於天上、地下與天堂的所有角落，以及其間的所有虛空。全能的主啊！見到您奇妙而讓人敬畏的形象，十方世界都畏懼而顫抖不已。

21. 「成群的天堂眾生也在行列之中，其中一些敬畏地兩掌合十；偉大的先知與能人則以讚歌頌揚您的榮耀，高呼：『萬歲！』

22. 「諸維生力量、眾星、火、地、空氣、天空、日月星辰與天堂；眾天使、宇宙的守護諸神、神聖的療癒者、諸風、父老們、天堂歌手們；以及成群的馬蒙（財神）崇拜者；還有惡人與聖人，全都大為驚愕。

23. 「最強大的主啊！在見了您有著各種不同面孔、無數的眼睛、四肢與駭人的嘴，這種種驚人形象後，我自己與十方世界都敬畏不已。

17. I see You with the crown, the scepter and the discus; a blaze of splendor. Scarce can I gaze on You, so radiant You are, glowing like the blazing fire, brilliant as the sun, immeasurable.

18. Imperishable art You, the Sole One worthy to be known, the priceless Treasure-house of the universe, the immortal Guardian of the Life Eternal, the Spirit Everlasting.

19. Without beginning, without middle and without end, infinite in power, Your arms all-embracing, the sun and moon Your eyes, Your face beaming with the fire of sacrifice, flooding the whole universe with light.

20. Alone You fill all the quarters of the sky, earth and heaven, and the regions between. O Almighty Lord! Seeing Your marvelous and awe-inspiring Form, the spheres tremble with fear.

21. The troops of celestial Beings enter into You, some invoking You in fear, with folded palms; the Great Seers and Adepts sing hymns to Your Glory, saying 'All Hail.'

22. The Vital Forces, the Major Stars, Fire, Earth, Air, Sky, Sun, Heaven, Moon and Planets; the Angels, the Guardians of the Universe, the divine Healers, the Winds, the Fathers, the Heavenly Singers; and hosts of Mammon-worshipers, demons as well as saints, are amazed.

23. Seeing Your stupendous Form, O Most Mighty! with its myriad faces, its innumerable eyes and limbs and terrible jaws, I myself and all the worlds are overwhelmed with awe.

24.「我看到您廣大身長，直至雲霄，發出五顏六色的光芒，張大嘴巴，眼冒火光，我嚇壞了。我的主啊！我的勇氣與內心的平靜都離我而去。

25.「我看到您許多駭人的嘴，彷如世界毀滅時的熊熊火焰，讓我不知身在何處，無處得安息。主啊！您是宇宙的歸宿，求您憐憫！

26.「持國王諸子、諸王公、毗濕摩、德羅那與卡爾納，還有我方陣營的諸將領；

27.「我看到他們一股腦兒衝進您有著許多可怕利牙的口中，慘不忍睹。有一些在您嘴邊就已血肉模糊，頭被壓成粉碎。

28.「正如氾濫之河水狂奔入海，這些英雄們——人中之菁英——也撲向您那些炙熱的口中。

29.「正如飛蛾撲火，唯有死亡一途，撲向您口中之眾人也唯有自取滅亡。

30.「您彷彿吞噬了十方，以火焰舔舐了世界。您的榮光填滿了整個宇宙；您的劇烈光芒壓得宇宙毫無招架之力。

31.「告訴我您到底是誰，為什麼會有這麼可怕的形象？強大的主啊！我向您禮敬。我祈求您，求您慈悲，並讓我看您原來的樣子。我不懂您的意思是什麼。」

24. When I see You, touching the Heavens, glowing with color, with open mouth and wide open fiery eyes, I am terrified. O my Lord! my courage and my peace of mind desert me.

25. When I see Your mouths with their fearful jaws like glowing fires at the dissolution of creation, I lose all sense of place; I find no rest. Be merciful, O Lord in whom this universe abides!

26. All these sons of Dhritarashtra, with the hosts of princes, Bhishma, Drona and Karna, as well as the other warrior chiefs belonging to our side;

27. I see them all rushing headlong into Your mouths, with terrible tusks, horrible to behold. Some are mangled between Your jaws, with their heads crushed to atoms.

28. As rivers in flood surge furiously to the ocean, so these heroes, the greatest among men, fling themselves into Your flaming mouths.

29. As moths fly impetuously to the flame, only to be killed, so these men rush into Your mouths to court their own destruction.

30. You seem to swallow up the worlds, to lap them in flame. Your glory fills the universe. Your fierce rays beat down upon it irresistibly.

31. Tell me then who You are, that wear this dreadful Form. I bow before You, O Mighty One! Have mercy, I pray, and let me see You as You were at first. I do not know what You intend.

32. 克里希納答：「我示現給你的，是我做為毀滅世界的毀滅者形象，其目的就是毀滅。你縱然努力，所有集結於此戰鬥的戰士都仍難逃一死。

33. 「束緊腰帶，起而戰鬥吧。征服敵人並享受王國的榮華。我已判定了他們的命運。成為我的工具吧，阿朱納！

34. 「德羅那、毗濕摩、勝車、卡爾納，以及其他英勇的戰士——我都已對他們做了宣判。消滅他們吧，起而戰鬥，無有畏懼。你的敵人將被擊潰。」

35. 山佳亞續言道：在聽了克里希納的話語後，阿朱納王子合十的雙手顫抖著，俯跪在主面前一再地敬禮，並且心中充滿敬畏，他聲音哽咽地再次向主言道。

36. 阿朱納道：「我的主！當世人歌頌您的榮耀時，他們很自然地感到歡欣喜悅；惡人害怕而紛飛四散，聖人則致上他們的敬意。

37. 「他們怎能不如此呢？啊！您是最最無上的自性（大我），比創世之諸神更偉大，是第一因，是無限者，是眾王之王，是宇宙的歸宿，是永不毀滅的；您既是存有也是非存有，而卻又超越了二者。

38. 「您是最初的上帝，是那亙古的，是宇宙的無上居所，是知曉者，是知識，是最終的歸處。您充滿了一切事物。您的形象是無限的。

Lord Shri Krishna replied:

32. I have shown Myself to you as the Destroyer who lays waste the world, and whose purpose now is destruction. In spite of your efforts, all these warriors gathered for battle shall not escape death.

33. Then gird up your loins and conquer. Subdue your foes and enjoy the kingdom in prosperity. I have already doomed them. Be My instrument, Arjuna!

34. Drona and Bhishma, Jayadratha and Karna, and other brave warriors – I have condemned them all. Destroy them; fight and fear not. Your foes shall be crushed.

Sanjaya continued:

35. Having heard these words from the Lord Shri Krishna, the Prince Arjuna, with folded hands trembling, prostrated himself and with choking voice, bowing down again and again, and overwhelmed with awe, once more addressed the Lord.

Arjuna said:

36. My Lord! It is natural that the world revels and rejoices when it sings the praises of Your glory; the demons fly in fear and the saints offer You their salutations.

37. How should they do otherwise? O Supremest Self, greater than the Powers of creation, the First Cause, Infinite, the Lord of Lords, the Home of the universe, Imperishable, Being and Not-Being, yet transcending both.

38. You are the Primal God, the Ancient, the Supreme Abode of this universe, the Knower, the Knowledge and the Final Home. You fill everything. Your form is infinite.

39.「您是風，是死亡，是火、水、月，是父親，是祖父。榮譽與榮耀歸於您千千萬萬次！我的主啊！我要一次又一次地向您致敬。

40.「我對著前方及四面八方的您禮敬，因您從十方將我全然含納在您裡面。您的力量是無限；您的莊嚴不可思量；您支撐一切萬物；是的，您就是一切。

41.「過去我輕率對您說的話語，把您只視為一位朋友，不經思索就親暱地稱呼您『克里希納啊！雅度之子啊！吾友啊！』，這都是因為沒有瞭解您的偉大。

42.「不論是在玩笑中、運動時、休息時、談話中或宴會中，獨處時或團體中，我為我在這些場合中曾羞辱您，請求您寬恕。您是獨一無二、無有匹比的！

43.「因您是所有會動與不會動之萬物的父親，您是可敬的，是師父中的師父！所有十方世界沒有人可與您匹配！無上的主啊！三界中怎麼可能有人能比得上您呢？[1]

44.「因此主啊！我匍匐跪拜在您面前。最敬愛的主啊！我向您禮拜，求您加持。只有您才能有如父親對於兒子、朋友對其朋友，以及愛人對他所摯愛的人一般地，對我如此容忍。

----

1 本句詩文的最後一句係參考伊斯瓦蘭與希瓦南達的英譯本而譯的，因為普羅希原譯較為簡略艱澀。

39. You are the Wind, You are Death, You are the Fire, the Water, the Moon, the Father and the Grandfather. Honor and glory to You a thousand and a thousand times! Again and again, salutation be to You, O my Lord!

40. Salutations to You in front and on every side, You who encompass me round about. Your power is infinite; Your majesty immeasurable; You uphold all things; yea, You Yourself are All.

41. Whatever I have said unto You in rashness, taking You only for a friend and addressing you as 'O Krishna! O Yadava! O Friend!' in thoughtless familiarity, not understanding Your greatness;

42. Whatever insult I have offered to You in jest, in sport or in repose, in conversation or at the banquet, alone or in a multitude, I ask Your forgiveness for them all, O You who are without an equal!

43. For You are the Father of all things movable and immovable, the Worshipful, the Master of Masters! In all the worlds there is none equal to You; how then superior' O You who stand alone, Supreme.

44. Therefore I prostrate myself before you, O Lord! Most Adorable! I salute You, I ask Your blessing. Only You can be trusted to bear with me, as father to son, as friend to friend, as lover to his beloved.

45.「我歡欣得見人們前所未見的；但主啊！我真的太害怕了。請回復到我所認識的形象吧。主啊！您是全宇宙的歸宿，我求您恩准。

46.「主啊！您有數不清的手臂與無數的形象，但我渴望見到您之前有著四隻手臂的另一個樣子，頭戴皇冠，手持權杖與鐵餅（武器）。」

47. 克里希納答：「我摯愛的朋友啊！只有透過我的恩典與力量，你才能夠見到這璀璨、遍及一切、無限、太初的景象。除你之外，從來就沒有人見過。

48.「俱盧族的大英雄啊！世人縱然研讀經文、獻祭或布施、儀式或嚴格的苦行，也不可能看到你所看到的這些。

49.「不要為這可怕的景象感到害怕或驚慌。拋開畏懼，再一次以喜悅之心看我平常的形象吧！」

50. 山佳亞續言道：對阿朱納說完了這些話後，克里希納再次地現示祂尋常的形象；並以溫和的聲調，柔和地安慰著驚恐害怕的阿朱納。

51. 阿朱納道：「我的主！看到您溫和的人類容貌後，我又恢復正常，再一次平靜了下來。」

45. I rejoice that I have seen what never man saw before; yet, O Lord! I am overwhelmed with fear. Please take again the Form I know. Be merciful, O Lord! You who are the Home of the whole universe.

46. I long to see You as You were before, with the crown, the scepter and the discus in Your hands; in Your other Form, with Your four hands, O You whose arms are countless and whose forms are infinite.

Lord Shri Krishna replied:
47. My beloved friend! It is only through My grace and power that you have been able to see this vision of splendor, the Universal, the Infinite, the Original. Never has it been seen by any but you.

48. Not by study of the scriptures, not by sacrifice or gift, not by ritual or rigorous austerity, is it possible for man on earth to see what you have seen, O foremost hero of the Kuru clan!

49. Be not afraid or bewildered by the terrible vision. Put away your fear and, with joyful mind, see Me once again in My usual Form.

Sanjaya continued:
50. Having thus spoken to Arjuna, Lord Shri Krishna showed Himself again in His accustomed form; and the Mighty Lord, in gentle tones, softly consoled him who lately trembled with fear.

Arjuna said:
51. Seeing You in Your gentle human form, my Lord, I am myself again, calm once more.

52. 克里希納答：「想要像你之前所看到的我的這些樣貌，是困難的。即便是最有權力的人求之也徒然不可得。

53.「縱然研讀經文、苦行、布施或獻祭，也不可能看到你所看到的我。

54.「只有透過努力不懈的誠心才能見到我、認識我；阿朱納啊！也唯有如此才能與我合而為一。

55.「每一行止都是為我而做，以我為最終的目標，唯獨只愛我而不憎恨任何人，我最親愛的孩子啊！只有這樣的人能了悟我！」

這就是聖靈的科學與自我認識的藝術、奧義書之一的聖典──《薄伽梵歌》中，克里希納與阿朱納王子對話的第十一章，名為「宇宙景象」。

Lord Shri Krishna replied:

52. It is hard to see this vision of Me that you have seen. Even the most powerful have longed for it in vain.

53. Not by study of the scriptures, or by austerities, not by gifts or sacrifices, is it possible to see Me as you have done.

54. Only by tireless devotion can I be seen and known; only thus can a man become one with Me, O Arjuna!

55. He whose every action is done for My sake, to whom I am the final goal, who loves Me only and hates no one – O my dearest Son! Only he can realize Me.

Thus, in the Holy Book the Bhagavad Gita, one of the Upanishads, in the Science of the Supreme Spirit, in the Art of Self-Knowledge, in the colloquy between the Divine Lord Shri Krishna and the Prince Arjuna, stands the eleventh chapter, entitled: The Cosmic Vision.

12

奉愛之道：
巴克提瑜伽

The Path of Love: Bhakti Yoga

本章的主題是「奉愛之道：巴克提瑜伽」。史密斯（1995）
說，巴克提瑜伽的目的是引導那潛藏在每個人心中的愛朝向
神（上帝）。因為生命的推動多出自情感而少發自理性，而在
充塞於人心中的各種情緒、情感中，愛是最強烈的（以「第四
道」的用語來說，就是多數的人是傾向「情感中心」的），因
此相對於其他的修行道路，奉愛之道有最多的追隨者。

奉愛之道，也稱虔誠瑜伽，是透過全心奉獻、信心與愛而
了悟上帝的一條道路，也是克里希納所讚賞的，祂在本章結尾
說：

「我實實在在地告訴你：喜愛我所教導的靈性智慧，信
心永遠不墜，整個人專注於我，這樣的人確實是我最摯愛
的。」（12:20）

這條信心與愛心的道路也是其他主要宗教 —— 尤其是
基督宗教 —— 所重視的。主耶穌說：「我實實在在地告訴你
們，信的人有永生。」（約翰福音 6:47）；〈哥林多前書〉中
說：「如今常存的有信，有望，有愛；這三樣，其中最大的是
愛。」（13:13）。在《華嚴經》中，釋迦牟尼佛也說：「信為道
源功德母，長養一切諸善根。」

但是對於身處造化之中的眾生，要怎樣才能有愛呢？因為
愛的本質就是「合一」，所以必須有「二」，才能有合一。母親
與孩子為二，所以才能有愛。我們（眾生）與上帝為二，所以
才能有愛，有合一的渴望。這也正是何以本章一開始，阿朱納

就對克里希納提出是否應以具有「位格」（人格化）的上帝來認識祂的主要原因。[1]

上主無所不在、無形無相，但對有限的眾生而言，卻必須在心中將無限的上帝具體化，才能有愛。的確，克里希納在本章中說得很清楚：

「……將注意力放在絕對者與不具位格上帝的人，會遭遇到較大的困境，因為對於擁有肉身的人而言，要以我是沒有肉身的方式來了悟我是困難的。」（12:5）

然而並不是每個人都能夠輕易地行奉愛之道。從靈性的角度來說，這恐怕與人過去生生世世的因果業力有關；從心理學的角度來看，則認為與人生命初期（嬰兒時期，或甚至是在母胎中）的經驗（尤其是關於父母的經驗）有絕大關係。在我們成長的過程中，與父母的關係是最接近「無條件」的，而這種經驗也最貼近我們與上帝的關係。（當然嚴格而言，所有的「關係」都是「替代品」，都是造化〔摩耶〕設計來「取代」上主無條件的愛的贗品。）然而世間的父母卻不是完美的上帝，因此如果一個人在生命的初期無法經驗到相當的安全與信賴，在其深層潛意識中，將也不容易與上帝有這樣的愛與信賴的關

1　位格一詞有其神學與哲學的歷史根源。尤煌傑（2001）指出，在哲學上，位格的最早定義是「理性本性的個別實體」，是由五世紀的哲學家波其武（Boethius）所定義的。神學家阿奎那（Thomas Aquinas）將這個詞進一步擴充，認為位格需具備實體、完美性、自己存在、和他者分離、理性本性等五個條件（尤煌傑，2001）；因此人是具有位格的。但稍後神學上的論辯則集中在於上帝（聖父、聖子、聖靈的三位一體，trinity）是否如人一般具有位格。

係（這也是造化業力使然）。

　　儘管如此，克里希納在本章中，強調我們應不斷地練習將心念與理智堅定地繫於祂（12:8-12:9）。皈依祂，遵循祂的教理，克己自制，並從心去捨棄一切，如此我們仍可享有祂所賜予的平安。

1. 阿朱納問道：「我的主！有些人試著以具有位格的上帝來認識您，有些人則以您是不具位格且永不毀滅的來崇敬您，這兩類人中，哪一類是比較好的信眾呢？」[2]

2. 克里希納答：「心念恆常繫於我，總是以堅定不移的信心（道心）與專注來敬拜我，這樣的人是最佳的。

3. 「有些人認知我是永不毀滅、無法命名、未顯化、無所不在、不可想像、原初的、永遠不變以及永恆的，他們以如是態度敬拜我；

4. 「他們克制感官，同等看待生命中的所有境遇，而且為所有眾生的福祉而工作，這樣的人確然會來到我這裡。

5. 「但如此將注意力放在絕對者與不具位格上帝的人，會遭遇到較大的困境，因為對於擁有肉身的人而言，要以我是沒有肉身的方式來了悟我是困難的。

6. 「誠然，有些人以行動臣服於我，冥想我，敬拜我，靜坐沉思時唯獨專注於我，在想法上對我毫無保留，

7. 「阿朱納啊！對這些人而言，我很快地就將他們自生死之大海中解救出來，因為他們的心是繫念於我的。

---

2 簡單地說，「位格」就是「人格化」。就本質而言，上主當然是無限而超越一切的，所以不會侷限於有限的「位格」；祂既是具有位格，也是不具位格。但是克里希納指出，對有限的眾生而言，以具位格的方式來了悟上帝會比較容易一些。

Arjuna asked:

1. My Lord! Which are the better devotees who worship You, those who try to know You as a Personal God, or those who worship You as Impersonal and Indestructible?

Lord Shri Krishna replied:

2. Those who keep their minds fixed on Me, who worship Me always with unwavering faith and concentration – these are the very best.

3. Those who worship Me as the Indestructible, the Undefinable, the Unmanifest, the Omnipresent, the Unthinkable, the Primeval, the Immutable and the Eternal;

4. Subduing their senses, viewing all conditions of life with the same eye, and working for the welfare of all beings, assuredly they come to Me.

5. But they who thus fix their attention on the Absolute and Impersonal encounter greater hardships, for it is difficult for those who possess a body to realize Me as without one.

6. Verily, those who surrender their actions to Me, who muse on Me, worship Me and meditate on Me alone, with no thought save of Me,

7. O Arjuna! I rescue them quickly from the ocean of life and death, for their minds are fixed on Me.

8.「因此將你的心念唯獨依靠於我，讓你的理智安住在我內；如此你也必然將全然地活於我內。

9.「但是如果你無法將你的心念堅定地繫於我，那麼我摯愛的朋友啊！你也要試著不斷地修持，努力去做。

10.「假若你不夠堅定，無法修持專注，那就對我獻身服侍吧：讓所有的行為都是為我而做，那麼你依舊可以達到你的目標。

11.「假如你過於軟弱，連這都做不到，那麼就皈依於我、尋求與我合一，並且藉由全然的克己自制，捨棄所有行為的果實。

12.「知識優於盲目的行動，靜坐冥想優於僅僅擁有知識，而對於行為果實之捨棄則又優於靜坐冥想。只要有捨棄，就有平安。

13.「對所有眾生無憎恨，親切而慈悲，不自私、不驕傲，在苦樂中都保有平和寧靜，而且是寬容的，

14.「總是滿足、心念中定、克己自制、果斷，把情感與理智都獻給我，這樣的信徒是我摯愛的。

15.「不傷害世人，也能不為世人所傷害，而且不為喜怒或畏懼所動，這樣的人是我所摯愛的。

8. Then let your mind cling only to Me, let your intellect abide in Me; and without doubt you shall live hereafter in Me alone.

9. But if you cannot fix your mind firmly on Me, then, My beloved friend! try to do so by constant practice.

10. And if you are not strong enough to practice concentration, then devote yourself to My service, do all your acts for My sake, and you shall still attain the goal.

11. And if you are too weak even for this, then seek refuge in union with Me, and with perfect self-control renounce the fruit of all your action.

12. Knowledge is superior to blind action, meditation to mere knowledge, renunciation of the fruit of action to meditation, and where there is renunciation, peace will follow.

13. He who is incapable of hatred towards any being, who is kind and compassionate, free from selfishness, without pride, equable in pleasure and in pain, and forgiving,

14. Always contented, self-centered, self-controlled, resolute, with mind and reason dedicated to Me, such a devotee of Mine is my beloved.

15. He who does not harm the world, and whom the world cannot harm, who is not carried away by any impulse of joy, anger or fear, such a one is My beloved.

16.「不期待什麼、純真、警醒、無分別、不受干擾，捨棄所有的主動行為，這樣的人是我所摯愛的。

17.「超越快樂與憎恨，無悲亦無求，好運、壞運都相同，這樣的人是我所摯愛的。

18.「對敵友都一視同仁，榮辱、冷熱、苦樂都等同接受，不迷戀任何事物，

19.「對毀譽無有分別，享受靜默，滿足於所有命運，沒有固定住所，心不動搖，而且誠心滿滿，這樣的人是我所摯愛的。

20.「我實實在在地告訴你：喜愛我教導的靈性智慧，信心永遠不墜，整個人專注於我，這樣的人確實是我最摯愛的。」

這就是聖靈的科學與自我認識的藝術、奧義書之一的聖典——《薄伽梵歌》中，克里希納與阿朱納王子對話的第十二章，名為「奉愛之道：巴克提瑜伽」。

16. He who expects nothing, who is pure, watchful, indifferent, unruffled, and who renounces all initiative, such a one is My beloved.

17. He who is beyond joy and hate, who neither laments nor desires, to whom good and evil fortunes are the same, such a one is My beloved.

18. He to whom friend and foe are alike, who welcomes equally honor and dishonor, heat and cold, pleasure and pain, who is enamored of nothing,

19. Who is indifferent to praise and censure, who enjoys silence, who is contented with every fate, who has no fixed abode, who is steadfast in mind and filled with devotion, such a one is My beloved.

20. Verily those who love the spiritual wisdom as I have taught, whose faith never fails, and who concentrate their whole nature on Me, they indeed are My most beloved.

Thus, in the Holy Book the Bhagavad Gita, one of the Upanishads, in the Science of the Supreme Spirit, in the Art of Self-Knowledge, in the colloquy between the Divine Lord Shri Krishna and the Prince Arjuna, stands the twelfth chapter, entitled: the Path of Love: Bhakti Yoga.

- Chapter -

13

物質與聖靈

Matter and Spirit

　　本章是很特殊的一章。在多數中英譯本中，都把本章命名為「場與場的知曉者」（field and knower of the field）。正如伊斯瓦蘭（1985，第 212 頁）所言，「場」這個字實際上是相當現代的一個字眼（尤其是從物理學的觀點來看；像是磁場、重力場等），因為「場」描述的是物質、能量、時空，乃至層層心智所擴展出來的連續體（continuum）。西方的物理學一直到愛因斯坦相對論的提出，才把物質與能量視為是不可分別的事物；但《薄伽梵歌》早就已經有了這樣的看法，甚至更進一步把物質與心智視為不可分別的；二者只是造化展現的不同面向罷了。[1]

　　在本章中，克里希納說我們的肉身就是「場」，而我們的自性就是「場的知曉者」（13:1）。但祂所說的場並不只侷限於肉身，事實上祂所說的場就是這個物質世界、造化；至於「場的知曉者」則是我們的自性，也就是菩盧薩。

　　普羅希在這個英譯本中，巧妙地以「活動場所」（playground；或譯「遊戲場」）來取代「場」；因為克里希納在這裡強調的場乃指肉身，以自性的活動場所來說明也頗為傳神。普羅希也以比較有基督宗教色彩的「聖靈」一詞來替代「自性」，如此也比較容易為歐美人士瞭解與接受。

1　愛因斯坦生命最後的幾十年將心力投入在「統一場論」的研究上，嘗試尋找一個一統的理論，含納、解釋宇宙所有的作用力（引力、電磁力、強弱作用力等），但並未成功。統一場論至今仍是物理學上待解之謎，更不用說是要解釋心靈的力量了。從更寬廣的角度來看，如果僅僅侷限於唯物、機械的眼光，恐怕永遠得不出最終的答案。

　　阿朱納問：「我的主！ 誰是上帝？何為造化？何謂物質？又何為自性？人們稱為智慧的究竟是什麼？什麼是值得去知曉的？我希望您為我解釋這些疑問。」

1. 克里希納答：「阿朱納啊！人的肉身是自性的活動場所；而那了知諸物質活動者，聖哲們稱之為自性。

2.「我是無所不在的自性，悠遊於物質的活動場所；有關物質以及那無所不知的自性的知識，就是智慧。

3.「何謂物質，它是由什麼構成的，它自何而來，又為何會變易？何謂自性，以及其力量為何？這些我現在將簡要地為你說明。

4.「先知們用各種方式，包括許多意義深遠且說理有力的讚歌與吠陀聖歌來歌頌它。

5.「五大基本元素（地、水、火、風與以太〔空〕）、個性、理智、神秘的生命力量、認知與行動的十種器官（十根）、意念，以及五類感官；[2]

6.「好惡、悲喜、同情、活力，以及對生命持續的執著；變易的物質基本上就是由這些組成的。

2　「認知與行動的十種器官」係指認知的「五知根」與行動的「五作根」，二者合稱「十根」。五類感官則指色、聲、香、味、觸等「五根境」。

Arjuna asked:

My Lord! Who is God and what is Nature; what is Matter and what is the Self; what is that they call Wisdom, and what is it that is worth knowing? I wish to have this explained.

Lord Shri Krishna replied:

1. O Arjuna! The body of man is the playground of the Self; and that which knows the activities of Matter, sages call the Self.

2. I am the Omniscient Self that abides in the playground of Matter; knowledge of Matter and of the all-knowing Self is wisdom.

3. What is called Matter, of what it is composed, whence it came, and why it changes, what the Self is, and what Its power – this I will now briefly set forth.

4. Seers have sung of It in various ways, in many hymns and sacred Vedic songs, weighty in thought and convincing in argument.

5. The five great fundamentals (earth, fire, air, water and ether), personality, intellect, the mysterious life force, the ten organs of perception and action, the mind and the five domains of sensation;

6. Desire, aversion, pleasure, pain, sympathy, vitality and the persistent clinging to life, these are in brief the constituents of changing Matter.

7.「謙遜、誠摯、不傷害（非暴力）、寬恕、正直、對師父的服侍、純真、堅定、克己自制；

8.「捨棄感官之樂、不驕傲、對生老病死四苦的正確瞭解；

9.「無分別、對性、子女與家庭都無戀著、不為福禍所動搖；

10.「專注於我，而且唯獨我，對我虔誠不移；喜好獨處，對社交漠不關心；

11.「不斷渴求關於自性的知識，並且思量有關偉大真理的教誨——此即為智慧；所有其餘的，皆是愚昧（無明）。

12.「現在我要告訴你那人們應當知曉的偉大真理，因為藉著它人們將可贏得不朽之極樂——那是無始，是永恆聖靈所在的我；既是無形無相，卻又非無形無相。

13.「到處都是『它』的手與腳、能見的眼睛、能想的頭腦、能說的嘴巴；『它』無處不聽見；『它』住於一切世界；『它』也含納這一切。[3]

14.「超越感官，卻又穿梭於所有的感官知覺。『它』不受任何事物束縛，卻又長養一切。不受造化三性影響，卻又享有造化三性的一切。

15.「『它』在眾生之內，卻又在眾生之外；既靜且動；細微不可辨；遙遠卻又總是在近旁。

3　這裡的「它」是指梵，即無上聖靈。

7. Humility, sincerity, harmlessness, forgiveness, rectitude, service of the Master, purity, steadfastness, self-control;

8. Renunciation of the delights of sense, absence of pride, right understanding of the painful problems of birth and death, of age and sickness;

9. Indifference; non-attachment to sex, progeny or home; equanimity in good fortune and in bad;

10. Unswerving devotion to Me, by concentration on Me and Me alone, a love for solitude, indifference to social life;

11. Constant yearning for the knowledge of Self, and pondering over the lessons of the great Truth – this is Wisdom, all else ignorance.

12. I will speak to you now of that great Truth which man ought to know, since by its means he will win immortal bliss; That which is without beginning, the Eternal Spirit which dwells in Me, neither with form, nor yet without it.

13. Everywhere are Its hands and Its feet; everywhere It has eyes that see, heads that think and mouths that speak; everywhere It listens; It dwells in all the worlds; It envelops them all.

14. Beyond the senses, It yet shines through every sense perception. Bound to nothing, It yet sustains everything. Unaffected by the Qualities, It still enjoys them all.

15. It is within all beings, yet outside; motionless yet moving; too subtle to be perceived; far away yet always near.

16.「既是所有眾生內不可分割的一部分，卻活生生地在眾生之外；『它』是萬物的長養者，是造物主，也同樣是毀滅者。

17.「『它』是眾光之光，非黑暗所能觸及。此一大智慧，是唯一值得知曉的，也是智慧唯獨所能教導的。『它』是一切眾生心中的當下。

18.「至此我已簡要地告訴你何謂物質，什麼是值得去了悟的自性，以及何謂智慧。獻身於我的人會瞭解，而且也必然會進入我之內。

19.「當知造化與上帝都是沒有起始的；而人們品行與其內在三性之不同，全是源自於造化。

20.「造化是造出因果的律則；上帝則是承受享有一切苦樂的源頭。

21.「住於造化中心的上帝，體驗由造化所造的三性；而祂與三性間之因緣，決定了祂所住的肉身是善或惡。

22.「因此在人的肉身中住著無上的上帝，祂能看見、允諾、長養、享受，是至高的上帝，是至高的自性。

23.「瞭解上帝、造化與造化三性的人，不論其生命之境遇如何，無須再降生塵世。

16. In all beings undivided, yet living in division, It is the upholder of all, Creator and Destroyer alike;

17. It is the Light of lights, beyond the reach of darkness; the Wisdom, the only thing that is worth knowing or that wisdom can teach; the Presence in the hearts of all.

18. Thus have I told you in brief what Matter is, and the Self worth realizing and what is Wisdom. He who is devoted to Me knows; and assuredly he will enter into Me.

19. Know further that Nature and God have no beginning; and that differences of character and quality have their origin in Nature only.

20. Nature is the Law which generates cause and effect; God is the source of the enjoyment of all pleasure and pain.

21. God dwelling in the heart of Nature experiences the Qualities which Nature brings forth; and His affinity toward the Qualities is the reason for His living in a good or evil body.

22. Thus in the body of man dwells the Supreme God: He who sees and permits, upholds and enjoys; the Highest God and the Highest Self.

23. He who understands God and Nature along with her Qualities, whatever be his condition in life, he comes not again to earth.

24.「有些人藉由靜坐冥想其內在之自性而了悟至上，有些人是藉由單純的理解（智慧之道），而有些人則是透過正行。

25.「同樣地，也有一些人並沒有直接得到知識，只是從別人處聽聞，但還是敬拜；那麼這些人，只要是忠實於教理，仍然可跨越死亡之海。

26.「不論是會動或不會動的事物，但凡有生命在其內，都是物質與聖靈的共同產物。

27.「能於眾生中見到至高上主，於腐朽的事物中見到不朽，這樣的人才是真正地看見。

28.「在一切萬物中都能無有分別地看到上主，其行動作為不但不會損及其屬靈的生命，反而會引導他到至福的境界。

29.「瞭解一切都只是造化的律則將行動導向結果，而自性從來就無為，這樣的人是了知真理的。

30.「看到形象各異的生命皆來自於『一』，自祂而生而長，這樣的人必然會尋得絕對者（上主）。

31.「王子啊！無上聖靈是無始的，也無三性，而且是不朽的；『它』雖然在肉身之內，但『它』並不作為，也不為作為所影響。

24. Some realize the Supreme by meditating, by its aid, on the Self within, others by pure reason, others by right action.

25. Others again, having no direct knowledge but only hearing from others, nevertheless worship, and they too, if true to the teachings, cross the sea of death.

26. Wherever life is seen in things movable or immovable, it is the joint product of Matter and Spirit.

27. He who can see the Supreme Lord in all beings, the Imperishable amid the perishable, he it is who really sees.

28. Beholding the Lord in all things equally, his actions do not mar his spiritual life but lead him to the height of Bliss.

29. He who understands that it is only the Law of Nature that brings action to fruition, and that the Self never acts, alone knows the Truth.

30. He who sees the diverse forms of life all rooted in the One, and growing forth from Him, he shall indeed find the Absolute.

31. The Supreme Spirit, O Prince! is without beginning, without Qualities and Imperishable, and though it be within the body, yet It does not act, nor is It affected by action.

32.「正如虛空，雖無所不在，但因其精微之本質而能不受影響；自性亦然，雖存於形象各異的生命中，仍保有其純然本性。

33.「猶如太陽普照大地，上主之光也同樣遍及寰宇。

34.「因此具慧眼的人看出物質與聖靈的分別，並了知生命如何自造化的律則中解脫，他們證得無上。」

這就是聖靈的科學與自我認識的藝術、奧義書之一的聖典——《薄伽梵歌》中，克里希納與阿朱納王子對話的第十三章，名為「物質與靈性」。

32. As space, though present everywhere, remains by reason of its subtlety unaffected, so the Self, though present in all forms, retains Its purity unalloyed.

33. As the one Sun illuminates the whole earth, so the Lord illumines the whole universe.

34. Those who with the eyes of wisdom thus see the difference between Matter and Spirit, and know how to liberate Life from the Law of Nature, they attain the Supreme.

Thus, in the Holy Book the Bhagavad Gita, one of the Upanishads, in the Science of the Supreme Spirit, in the Art of Self-Knowledge, in the colloquy between the Divine Lord Shri Krishna and the Prince Arjuna, stands the thirteenth chapter, entitled: Matter and Spirit.

14

造化三性

The Three Qualities

　　本章談論形塑內在心理世界與外在物質世界的基本力量——造化（普拉克里提，prakriti）的本質，也就是造化三性。克里希納在這一章中，簡短地為阿朱納解說這三種屬性力量的差別。在稍後第十七與第十八章中，則進一步從信念、獻祭、理智、職責，甚至是飲食與修行等多方面，說明造化三性消長所呈現的不同面貌。讀者也可參考〈導讀〉中的補充說明。

　　克里希納雖指出處於造化中的我們無法逃脫造化三性的影響，但祂更強調的是，我們當瞭解，這三性的消長變化，不論高低，都是造化律則的所為。我們應當接受來到我們面前的所有一切，不論苦樂；也平等對待所有眾生，不論尊卑親疏或敵友，如此方能超越造化的束縛。當然，更重要的，是時時刻刻地專注於上主；藉由將一切供養上主的無我奉獻，我們將能了脫生死，與永恆上主合一。

1. 克里希納續言道：「現在我將為你揭示那超越知識的智慧，聖哲們藉由證得此智慧而臻至圓滿之境。

2. 「聖哲們智慧俱足，並了悟我的神聖，因此在每次宇宙重造的循環週期伊始，他們不用再生；同樣地當宇宙解離時，他們也不受影響。

3. 「王子啊！永恆的宇宙是我的子宮，我在其中灑下種子，眾生於是從中誕生。

4. 「卓越的昆蒂之子啊！不論人從誰而生，都是聖靈懷胎，而我是其父親。

5. 「純真、熱情與無明是自造化律則而來的三性質。它們束縛了眾生內在的自由聖靈。

6. 「無罪的人啊！三者中，純真是潔亮、強壯而堅韌的，因著其對幸福與開悟的渴求而把人束縛住。

7. 「熱情，由對享樂與執著的欲望所驅使，因著其對行動的喜愛而把靈魂束縛住。

8. 「無明（愚昧），是黑暗的產物，以環環相扣的愚行、懶惰與昏睡來蒙蔽眾生的感官。

9. 「純真帶來快樂，熱情帶來激動，至於那迷惑智慧的無明，則導致失敗的人生。

Lord Shri Krishna continued:

1. Now I will reveal unto you the Wisdom which is beyond knowledge, by attaining which the sages have reached Perfection.

2. Dwelling in Wisdom and realizing My Divinity, they are not born again when the universe is re-created at the beginning of every cycle, nor are they affected when it is dissolved.

3. The eternal Cosmos is My womb, in which I plant the seed, from which all beings are born, O Prince!

4. O illustrious son of Kunti! Through whatever wombs men are born, it is the Spirit Itself that conceives, and I am their Father.

5. Purity, Passion and Ignorance are the Qualities which the Law of Nature brings forth. They fetter the free Spirit in all beings.

6. O Sinless One! Of these, Purity, being luminous, strong and invulnerable, binds one by its yearning for happiness and illumination.

7. Passion, engendered by thirst for pleasure and attachment, binds the soul through its fondness for activity.

8. But Ignorance, the product of darkness, stupefies the senses in all embodied beings, binding them by chains of folly, indolence and lethargy.

9. Purity brings happiness, Passion commotion, and Ignorance, which obscures wisdom, leads to a life of failure.

10.「王子啊！當純真戰勝熱情與無明，純真就顯現；當熱情戰勝了純真與無明，熱情就顯現；而當無明戰勝純真與熱情，無明就顯現。

11.「當知識之光從身體的竅門透出來，那就必然是純真佔了優勢。

12.「印度之雄啊！貪婪、行動的推力，與行動的起始本身，都是由熱情支配的。

13.「俱盧族之寵啊！黑暗、滯塞、愚昧與沉迷，都是無明主導下的結果。

14.「當純真戰勝，則靈魂在離開肉身時會前往純淨的國度——那裡是認識至高上主的人所居住的地方。

15.「當熱情佔上風時，靈魂會再轉世到那些喜愛行動作為的人群之中；當無明主導時，靈魂會進入無明者的子宮中。

16.「人們說善行的果實是無瑕且滿覆純真，熱情的結果是苦難，而無明的結果是黑暗。

17.「純真帶來智慧，熱情帶來貪欲，無明則是帶來愚昧、沉迷與黑暗。

18.「當純真佔優勢時，人會進化；若熱情佔優勢，他不進也不退；若無明佔優勢，則會迷失。

10. O Prince! Purity prevails when Passion and Ignorance are overcome; Passion, when Purity and Ignorance are overcome; and Ignorance when it overcomes Purity and Passion.

11. When the light of knowledge gleams forth from all the gates of the body, then be sure that Purity prevails.

12. O best of Indians! Avarice, the impulse to act, and the beginning of action itself, are all due to the dominance of Passion.

13. Darkness, stagnation, folly and infatuation are the result of the domination of Ignorance, O joy of the Kuru clan!

14. When Purity prevails, the soul on quitting the body passes on to the pure regions where live those who know the Highest.

15. When Passion prevails, the soul is reborn among those who love activity; when Ignorance rules, it enters the wombs of the ignorant.

16. They say the fruit of a meritorious action is spotless and full of Purity; the outcome of Passion is misery, and of Ignorance darkness.

17. Purity engenders Wisdom, Passion avarice, and Ignorance folly, infatuation and darkness.

18. When Purity is in the ascendant, the man evolves; when Passion, he neither evolves nor degenerates; when Ignorance, he is lost.

19.「人一旦瞭解了一切都是造化三性之所為，此外別無其他，並能體認到那超越這一切的（上主），那麼他就證得了我的神聖本質。

20.「當靈魂超越了造化三性——也就是物質存在的真正肇因，那麼他就從生死與老苦中解脫，將狂飲不死的甘露。」

21. 阿朱納問道：「我的主！超越了造化三性的人，有什麼可辨認的徵兆呢？他們的行為如何？他們是怎麼生活才能超越三性的呢？」

22. 克里希納答：「王子啊！不論三性何者出現，他們不逃避；而不在時也不追尋；

23.「維持無分別的態度，不為三性所騷動，了悟一切皆為三性所為，並保持寧靜；

24.「接受所有到來的苦樂，中定於自性，土石與金玉對其而言無異，無有好惡，堅定不移，對毀譽漠不關心；

25.「同等看待榮辱，愛朋友也愛敵人，捨棄所有主動行為，這樣的人就是超越造化三性的。

26.「以堅定不移之道心服侍我，且唯獨我，這樣的人將克服造化三性，而且與永恆合一。

19. As soon as a man understands that it is only the Qualities which act and nothing else, and perceives That which is beyond, he attains My divine nature.

20. When the soul transcends the Qualities, which are the real cause of physical existence, then, freed from birth and death, from old age and misery, he quaffs the nectar of immortality.

Arjuna asked:

21. My Lord! By what signs can he who has transcended the Qualities be recognized? How does he act? How does he live beyond them?

Lord Shri Krishna replied:

22. O Prince! He who shuns not the Quality which is present, and longs not for that which is absent;

23. He who maintains an attitude of indifference, who is not disturbed by the Qualities, who realizes that it is only they who act, and remains calm;

24. Who accepts pleasure or pain as it comes, is centered in his Self, to whom a piece of clay or a stone or gold are the same, who neither likes nor dislikes, who is steadfast, indifferent alike to praise or censure;

25. Who looks equally upon honor and dishonor, loves friends and foes alike, abandons all initiative, such is he who transcends the Qualities.

26. And he who serves Me and only Me, with unfaltering devotion, shall overcome the Qualities, and become One with the Eternal.

27.「因為我是聖靈的居所，是永生、永恆正義與無限喜樂的
　　活水源頭。」

這就是聖靈的科學與自我認識的藝術、奧義書之一的聖
典——《薄伽梵歌》中，克里希納與阿朱納王子對話的第十四
章，名為「造化三性」。

27. For I am the Home of the Spirit, the continual Source of immortality, of eternal Righteousness and of infinite Joy.

Thus, in the Holy Book the Bhagavad Gita, one of the Upanishads, in the Science of the Supreme Spirit, in the Art of Self-Knowledge, in the colloquy between the Divine Lord Shri Krishna and the Prince Arjuna, stands the fourteenth chapter, entitled: The Three Qualities.

– Chapter –

15

上主

The Lord God

　　在這一章的開頭，克里希納把這個世界，或者說是我們的俗世生命，比喻為一棵上下顛倒的菩提樹。這棵枝葉交錯的樹，其形象有如我們的神經系統，其錯綜複雜的神經細胞，自腦部延伸至全身，接收來自身體感官的訊號。猶太教的神秘教派卡巴拉（Kabbalah），以及創立於十九世紀中葉的巴哈伊教（Baha'i Faith），都有類似的生命之樹的比喻。[1]

　　克里希納在本章中說：

　　「我永恆自性的小小一部分──也就是此宇宙的生命──悠遊於源自造化的六根（心是其中最後者）之間。」（15:7）

　　有些人對於上主將祂的「小小一部分」變成我們的生命（自性）感到困惑，因為自性既從上主「分離」出來，那自性豈能又與上主的永恆自性等同呢？克里希納既說祂是自性，也說祂超越自性，這豈不矛盾嗎？顯然，文字語言是有限的，而頭腦也同樣是有限的。以有限去思考無限，當然不得其解。

　　一個簡單的比喻或許有助於理解這個問題。這就好像我們自己設計了一個線上遊戲，然後自己登錄上線去玩。但又一再地忘掉帳號、密碼，所以就同時不斷地以新的帳號、密碼登錄上線去玩。（玩家沒有親自在場時，電腦系統會依循一些規則自動執行；每隔一段時間也會讓玩家「登出」、「下線」。）看

1　巴哈伊教認為這株樹的根源與主幹就是世世代代示現於此世界的上主，祂的追隨者就是枝葉，而文明就是樹上所結的果實所滋養的。不同於生命之樹的，還有知識之樹；前者代表非二元的靈性世界，而後者則是有善惡的二元物質世界（見 http://en.wikipedia.org/wiki/Tree_of_life.）。

起來，好像線上有很多不同的使用者在線上玩，事實上都只是同一個人。

　　線上遊戲、電腦系統就是造化；遊戲、系統的「規則」，就是造化三性組合而成的造化律則（業力法則）。每個使用者帳號都是自我（有限的小我），而真正操弄著鍵盤滑鼠、玩著遊戲的主人，就是自性。所以說「自性從上主『分離』出來」只是文字語言有限下的一種說法，並非真相。

1. 克里希納續言:「此非凡世界,既無常又永恆,有如一棵樹(菩提樹),但其根源(種子)在上,達於至上;其枝幹交錯往下,深植於塵世。眾經典是其葉子。瞭解此說法者,是真知者。

2. 「它的枝幹往上下四方伸展,從造化三性中萃取養分;它的芽是感官對象;它的根部則深植土中,依循造化之律則,左右著人的生死輪迴。

3. 「除非以不執著的利斧,將這株深扎於塵土的樹從根斬斷,否則於此塵世,其真正形象——不論是源頭或是終尾——都是不可知的,其力量也同樣地不可解。

4. 「在它的背後,就是道之所在,只要找到它,就不用再回來——那是遠古以前,創造此宇宙的原初上帝之所在。[2]

5. 「無有驕傲與妄念,克服了對感官事物的喜愛;捨棄欲望、專注於自性,不再被苦樂等二元對立的感官感受反覆煎熬;如此之智者證得永恆之境。

6. 「日、月或火的光都無法到達那裡。阿朱納啊!一旦到達那裡,就不用再回來,因為那裡是我的天堂住所!

7. 「我永恆自性的小小一部分——也就是此宇宙的生命——悠遊於源自造化的六根(心是其中最後者)之間。

---

2 這裡的「道」在普羅希的譯文中是大寫的 Path。

Lord Shri Krishna continued:

1. This phenomenal creation, which is both ephemeral and eternal, is like a tree, but having its seed above in the Highest, and its ramifications on this earth below. The scriptures are its leaves, and he who understands this, knows.

2. Its branches shoot upwards and downwards, deriving their nourishment from the Qualities; its buds are the objects of sense; and its roots, which follow the Law causing man's regeneration and degeneration, pierce downwards into the soil.

3. In this world its true form is not known, neither its origin nor its end, and its strength is not understood, until the tree with its roots striking deep into the earth is hewn down by the sharp axe of non-attachment.

4. Beyond lies the Path, from which, when found, there is no return. This is the Primal God from whence this ancient creation has sprung.

5. The wise attain Eternity when, freed from pride and delusion, they have conquered their love for the things of sense; when, renouncing desire and fixing their gaze on the Self, they have ceased to be tossed to and fro by the opposing sensations, like pleasure and pain.

6. Neither sun, moon, nor fire shines there. Those who go thither never come back. For, O Arjuna! that is My Celestial Home.

7. It is only a very small part of My Eternal Self, which is the life of this universe, drawing round itself the six senses, the mind the last, which have their source in Nature.

8.「至高上主進入或離開一個肉身，是祂將這些感官（六根）聚集並攜帶著步上旅程，就如同風吹拂過花朵，也會帶走其香氣一樣。

9.「祂是眼、耳、鼻、舌、身的覺知，也是心念（意）的覺知，而且覺知事物的樂趣也同屬於祂。

10.「無明者不明瞭：生就是祂臨在，死就是祂離開；他們也不知道是祂在體驗由造化三性而來的快樂。唯有慧眼才能看清這一切。

11.「精進之聖人在內在找到祂，但愚昧者則不然，因為他們不論多麼努力，都無法控制自己的意念。

12.「當知曉：照亮世界的太陽之光、月亮之光，以及火焰之光，全部都自我而生。

13.「我進入此世界，以我之能，將生命賦予我的所有創造物；而且藉著清涼的月光，我滋養了植物。

14.「我化為生命之火，穿梭於眾生軀體之內；調和其上行氣與下行氣之生命流，消化各種食物。

15.「我為眾生所衷心愛戴；記憶、智慧與明辨能力都來自於我。我就是眾經典中所要了悟的祂；是我啟發了經典中的智慧，而我瞭解其中所揭示的真理。

8. When the Supreme Lord enters a body or leaves it, He gathers these senses together and travels on with them, as the wind gathers perfume while passing through the flowers.

9. He is the perception of the ear, the eye, the touch, the taste and the smell, yea and of the mind also; and the enjoyment of the things which they perceive is also His.

10. The ignorant do not see that it is He who is present in life and who departs at death or even that it is He who enjoys pleasure through the Qualities. Only the eye of wisdom sees.

11. The saints with great effort find Him within themselves; but not the unintelligent, who in spite of every effort cannot control their minds.

12. Remember that the Light which, proceeding from the sun, illumines the whole world, and the Light which is in the moon, and that which is in the fire also, all are born of me.

13. I enter this world and animate all My creatures with My vitality; and by My cool moonbeams I nourish the plants.

14. Becoming the fire of life, I pass into their bodies and, uniting with the vital streams of Prana and Apana, I digest the various kinds of food.

15. I am enthroned in the hearts of all; memory, wisdom and discrimination owe their origins to Me. I am He who is to be realized in the scriptures; I inspire their wisdom and I know their truth.

16.「造化有兩面：一是會毀滅的，另一是不會毀滅的。所有塵世之生命皆屬於前者，而不變易的元素（聖靈）則屬於後者。

17.「但比所有這些都更高的，是我——是至高上帝、絕對自性、永恆之上主，我遍布十方世界，也維繫著所有一切。

18.「那超越永恆與非永恆的是我——經典與聖哲稱我為無上人格、至高上帝。

19.「眼睛不被蒙蔽的人看到我是上帝，了知一切需要瞭解的，而且總是全心地敬拜我。

20.「無罪的人啊！我已把最奧秘的知識揭示予你。瞭解的人由此獲得智慧，生命臻至圓滿。」

這就是聖靈的科學與自我認識的藝術、奧義書之一的聖典《薄伽梵歌》中，克里希納與阿朱納王子對話的第十五章，名為「上主」。

16. There are two aspects in Nature: the perishable and the imperishable. All life in this world belongs to the former, the unchanging element belongs to the latter.

17. But higher than all am I, the Supreme God, the Absolute Self, the Eternal Lord, who pervades the worlds and upholds them all.

18. Beyond comparison of the Eternal with the non-eternal am I, Who am called by scriptures and sages the Supreme Personality, the Highest God.

19. He who with unclouded vision sees Me as the Lord God, knows all there is to be known, and always shall worship Me with his whole heart.

20. Thus, O Sinless One! I have revealed to you this most mystic knowledge. He who understands gains wisdom and attains the consummation of life.

Thus, in the Holy Book the Bhagavad Gita, one of the Upanishads, in the Science of the Supreme Spirit, in the Art of Self-Knowledge, in the colloquy between the Divine Lord Shri Krishna and the Prince Arjuna, stands the fifteenth chapter, entitled: The Lord God.

16

神聖與邪惡

The Divine and Demoniac Civilizations

　　在這一章中，克里希納以罕見的強烈口吻，批評邪惡品質。祂敘述的這些邪惡品質，很貼切地描述了主導支配著今日世界的唯物主義與資本主義思維。這種唯物的、不可知論者的思維是危險的，因為在他們的眼中，只有肉眼可見的物質世界才是真實的，靈性則是虛無縹緲、痴人說夢；對他們而言，生命是沒有意義的，因而可悲地自甘墮落於物欲的享受之中。

　　除了這種「粗糙」的邪惡品質外，克里希納還提到另一種較微細的邪惡品質，也就是「我慢」。修行的陷阱之一就是當有一些靈性體驗或心得，就心生我慢，認為自己比其他人高等。這種自命不凡的我執，同樣導向墮落與生死輪迴，不可不慎。

1. 克里希納續言道:「無懼、清淨生活、無間斷地專注於智慧、喜捨、克己自制、有獻祭精神、常習經文、苦行、真誠,

2. 「無傷害(非暴力)、真實、無怒、捨棄、知足、直率、慈悲對待眾生、不貪、謙遜有禮、堅定,

3. 「英勇、寬恕、剛毅、純真、無有憎恨與虛榮;阿朱納啊!這些都是擁有上帝品質的人所具備的。

4. 「虛偽、驕慢無禮、殘酷以及愚昧,都是生而邪惡的人所擁有的非上帝品質。

5. 「上帝品質導向解脫,非上帝(邪惡)品質通往束縛。王子啊!別擔憂,你是有上帝品質的。

6. 「所有眾生分兩類:神聖的與邪惡的。我已經描述了前者,現在我將說明後者。

7. 「邪惡者既不知如何作為,也不知如何捨棄。他們既不純真也不真實。他們不瞭解正確的行為準則。

8. 「他們說宇宙誕生於意外——既無上帝也無目的可言。生命是性的結合所創造的,僅僅是淫慾的產物罷了。

9. 「如是思維,這些墮落的靈魂,這些人類的敵人——智慧不足,行為怪異——來此世界唯有破壞。

Lord Shri Krishna continued:

1. Fearlessness, clean living, unceasing concentration on wisdom, readiness to give, self-control, a spirit of sacrifice, regular study of the scriptures, austerities, candor,

2. Harmlessness, truth, absence of wrath, renunciation, contentment, straightforwardness, compassion towards all, uncovetousness, courtesy, modesty, constancy,

3. Valour, forgiveness, fortitude, purity, freedom from hate and vanity; these are his who possesses the Godly Qualities, O Arjuna!

4. Hypocrisy, pride, insolence, cruelty, ignorance belong to him who is born of the godless qualities.

5. Godly qualities lead to liberation; godless to bondage. Do not be anxious, Prince! You have the Godly qualities.

6. All beings are of two classes: Godly and godless. The Godly I have described; I will now describe the other.

7. The godless do not know how to act or how to renounce. They have neither purity nor truth. They do not understand the right principles of conduct.

8. They say that the universe is an accident with no purpose and no God. Life is created by sexual union, a product of lust and nothing else.

9. Thinking thus, these degraded souls, these enemies of mankind – whose intelligence is negligible and whose deeds are monstrous – come into the world only to destroy.

10.「沉溺於永不厭足的熱情中，虛偽、自負且傲慢，滿懷基於妄念的錯誤觀念，他們的所作所為，只為實現個人的邪惡目的。

11.「熱衷於邪惡的諸種作為，至死方休；視欲望的滿足為最高目標，其餘皆視而不見；

12.「他們深陷於各種空想之中，成為熱情與憤怒的奴隸，並且積聚不義之財，只為了迎合其感官欲望。

13.「今天我要得到這個，明天我要滿足另一個欲望；這個錢財是我的，其餘的不用多久也會是我的；

14.「我殺了一個敵人，其餘的我也要殺掉；我是值得享有這一切的，我是萬能，我是完美、有權勢，又快樂的；

15.「我富有，出身好，誰能與我相較？我會獻祭，我會給予，我會付出──而且我享受這一切。這些人就是如此地被無明蒙蔽。

16.「他們被衝突的想法所惑，陷於欲望的羅網，且沉迷於熱情，因而墜入恐怖的地獄之中。

17.「自負、固執、自恃富有、傲慢無理，他們自命不凡，蔑視禮法。

18.「他們吹噓權勢且極度自負，為貪淫與嗔怒所左右，這些邪惡之人厭惡在他們內在的我，因為我也在眾生之內。

10. Giving themselves up to insatiable passions, hypocritical, self-sufficient and arrogant, cherishing false conceptions founded on delusion, they work only to carry out their own unholy purposes.

11. Poring anxiously over evil resolutions, which only end in death; seeking only the gratification of desire as the highest goal; seeing nothing beyond;

12. Caught in the toils of a hundred vain hopes, the slaves of passion and of wrath, they accumulate hoards of unjust wealth, only to pander to their sensual desire.

13. This have I gained today; tomorrow I will gratify another desire; this wealth is mine now, the rest shall be mine ere long;

14. I have slain one enemy, I will slay the others also; I am worthy to enjoy, I am the Almighty, I am perfect, powerful and happy;

15. I am rich, I am well-bred; who is there to compare with me? I will sacrifice, I will give, I will pay – and I will enjoy. Thus blinded by ignorance.

16. Perplexed by discordant thoughts, entangled in the snares of desire, infatuated by passion, they sink into the horrors of hell.

17. Self-conceited, stubborn, rich, proud and insolent, they make a display of their patronage, disregarding the rules of decency.

18. Puffed up by power and inordinate conceit, swayed by lust and wrath, these wicked people hate Me who am within them, as I am within all.

19.「這些憎恨我又殘酷的人，是人類的渣滓，我判他們不斷地輪迴於悲慘邪惡之中。

20.「一再輪迴，生生世世為妄念所困。王子啊！他們無法到我這裡，而只會一再地墜落到更低等的生命型態之中。

21.「通往地獄之門有三：貪、嗔與淫。它們會毀滅自性，要避開它們。

22.「這些都是通往黑暗之門；避開它們，就可確保自身的福祉，而且最終也會獲得解脫。

23.「但忽略經典的指示，而只聽從於熱情的使喚，這樣的人無法達到圓滿、幸福與最終的目標。

24.「因此每當你對一事該為或不該為有所疑惑時，讓經典引導你的行為吧。你當全心全意依經典之教導而行。」

這就是聖靈的科學與自我認識的藝術、奧義書之一的聖典——《薄伽梵歌》中，克里希納與阿朱納王子對話的第十六章，名為「聖潔與邪惡」。

19. Those who thus hate Me, who are cruel, the dregs of mankind, I condemn them to a continuous, miserable and godless rebirth.

20. So reborn, they spend life after life, enveloped in delusion. And they never reach Me, O Prince! but degenerate into still lower forms of life.

21. The gates of hell are three: lust, wrath and avarice. They destroy the Self. Avoid them.

22. These are the gates which lead to darkness; if a man avoids them he will ensure his own welfare, and in the end will attain his liberation.

23. But he who neglects the commands of the scriptures and follows the promptings of passion, he does not attain perfection, happiness or the final goal.

24. Therefore whenever there is doubt whether you should do a thing or not, let the scriptures guide your conduct. In the light of the scriptures should you labor the whole of your life.

Thus, in the Holy Book the Bhagavad Gita, one of the Upanishads, in the Science of the Supreme Spirit, in the Art of Self-Knowledge, in the colloquy between the Divine Lord Shri Krishna and the Prince Arjuna, stands the sixteenth chapter, entitled: Divine and Demonic Civilization.

17

信仰三別

The Threefold Faith

　　在這一章中，克里希納從人的三性談論他們在信仰上的不同。這裡的信仰（梵文為 shraddha）並不純粹指宗教上的信仰，反而是指深植我們心中，而我們未曾有疑的信念（beliefs）。[1] 這些信念由價值觀、偏見等等構成；以近代西方心理學的用語來說，所有構成我們潛意識的內容（包括個人潛意識與集體潛意識），都是我們的信念與信仰。驅使我們生命的動力，主要來自潛意識，而不是意識。這就是為什麼克里希納說，人是由其信仰（信念）所造就的（17:3）。

　　人因造化三性的不同，因此其信念也都有所差異，這表現在宗教上是指信仰、食物的偏好、獻祭、苦行、布施等等。克里希納所說的苦行，並不是折磨自己的身體，而更是泛指身、口、意上的潔淨與修持。

　　雖然克里希納在這裡似乎盛讚純真的信仰，但在本章最後一部分，祂也提醒我們不論是獻祭、苦行、布施，或從事所有任何事宜，都應頌持永恆聖靈的三聖號 ——「唵」（O$_M$）、「沓」（T$_{AT}$）、「薩」（S$_{AT}$），並將一切作為供養，獻給上主。

1　在翻譯上，我們仍沿用英文的翻譯，譯為「信仰」（faith），但要提醒這裡其實更有信念的意思。

1. 阿朱納問道：「我的主！有些人未依經典進行獻祭，但內在
卻有信仰，他們的情況如何？這樣做是出於純真、熱情、
還是無明？」

2. 克里希納答道：「人生而具有自造化三性之一而來的信
仰——也就是純真、熱情與無明。現在且聽我訴說。

3. 「人的信仰遵循著他的本性。人天生就是充滿信仰的。事實
上，人就是由他的信仰造就的。

4. 「純真者敬拜真上帝，熱情者敬拜財富與神通之諸神，無明
者則敬拜死神與自然界的低等神祇。

5. 「未依經典之指示而修持苦行，被虛偽與自大奴役，以及因
欲望與熱情的猛烈侵襲而激動的人，

6. 「這樣的人是無明的。他們折磨身體的器官，也騷擾了住在
他們內在的我。當知他們是邪惡的信徒。

7. 「正如獻祭、苦行與布施的方式各有不同，人們享用的食物
也分三類。且聽它們有何區別。

8. 「延長壽命，並能增進純淨、活力、健康、喜悅與幸福的食
物是可口、寬慰、實在，並令人愉悅的。這是純真者所喜
愛的。

9. 「內在由熱情所支配的人喜歡苦、酸、鹹、過熱、辛辣，以
及又乾又焦的食物。這些食物造成不快、悔恨與疾病。

Arjuna asked:

1. My Lord! Those who do acts of sacrifice, not according to the scriptures but nevertheless with implicit faith, what is their condition? Is it one of Purity, of Passion or of Ignorance?

Lord Shri Krishna replied:

2. Man has an inherent faith in one or another of the Qualities - Purity, Passion and Ignorance. Now listen.

3. The faith of every man conforms to his nature. By nature he is full of faith. He is in fact what his faith makes him.

4. The Pure worship the true God; the Passionate, the powers of wealth and magic; the Ignorant, the spirits of the dead and of the lower orders of nature.

5. Those who practice austerities not commanded by scripture, who are slaves to hypocrisy and egotism, who are carried away by the fury of desire and passion.

6. They are ignorant. They torment the organs of the body; and they harass Me also, who lives within. Know that they are devoted to evil.

7. The food which men enjoy is also threefold, like the ways of sacrifice, austerity and almsgiving. Listen to the distinction.

8. The foods that prolong life and increase purity, vigor, health, cheerfulness and happiness are those that are delicious, soothing, substantial and agreeable. These are loved by the Pure.

9. Those in whom Passion is dominant like foods that are bitter, sour, salt, over-hot, pungent, dry and burning. These produce unhappiness, repentance and disease.

10.「無明者喜愛腐壞、不營養、腐臭、不潔的食物，以及他人與不潔淨者所吃剩的食物。

11.「如果獻祭是依循經典的指示，不貪想其報償，而是內心認定是職責所在，那麼這樣的獻祭就是純真的。

12.「雅利安人之傑啊！如果是為了其結果，或是為了自我炫耀而行獻祭，這樣的獻祭就是熱情的產物。

13.「違反經典指示，沒有誦經，也沒有布施食物或錢財，而且也沒有信仰，這樣的獻祭是無明的產物。

14.「敬拜上帝與師父，尊敬祭師與經師；純真、正直、節制，與非暴力（無傷害）——所有這些都是『身』（身體）的苦行。

15.「言語上不傷人、真實，且宜人而有益，並恆常研讀經典——這是『口』（言語）的苦行。

16.「沉著、仁慈、靜默、自制與純淨——這是『意』（意念）的苦行。

17.「以信心執行此三類苦行，且不考慮其果報，可算是真正的純真。

18.「苦行若是伴隨著虛偽，或是為了自我炫耀、媚俗或虛榮而行，這樣的苦行來自熱情，其結果必然是可疑而短暫的。

10. The Ignorant love food which is stale, not nourishing, putrid and corrupt, the leavings of others and unclean.

11. Sacrifice is Pure when it is offered by one who does not covet the fruit thereof, when it is done according to the commands of scripture, and with implicit faith that the sacrifice is a duty.

12. Sacrifice which is performed for the sake of its results, or for self-glorification – that, O best of Aryans! is the product of Passion.

13. Sacrifice that is contrary to scriptural command, that is unaccompanied by prayers or gifts of food or money, and is without faith – that is the product of Ignorance.

14. Worship of God and the Master; respect for the preacher and the philosopher; purity, rectitude, continence and harmlessness – all this is physical austerity.

15. Speech that hurts no one, that is true, is pleasant to listen to and beneficial, and the constant study of the scriptures – this is austerity in speech.

16. Serenity, kindness, silence, self-control and purity – this is austerity of mind.

17. These threefold austerities performed with faith, and without thought of reward, may truly be accounted Pure.

18. Austerity coupled with hypocrisy or performed for the sake of self-glorification, popularity or vanity, comes from Passion, and its result is always doubtful and temporary.

19.「依妄念行苦行，伴隨著巫術，或者是帶給己身或他人折磨，這樣的苦行可說是來自無明。

20.「布施而不思回報，而是以因時、因地、因人之所需而責無旁貸的信念為之——這樣的布施是純真。

21.「若是為其所帶來之果報，或是為求回報，或是心有勉強——這樣的布施真可說是來自熱情。

22.「布施的時空不當、對象不對，或心存不敬或蔑視——這樣的布施是來自無明。

23.「『唵』、『沓』、『薩』是永恆聖靈的三聖號；吠陀經典、儀式、獻祭，皆自此而出。

24.「因此瞭解聖靈者在進行經典所述的獻祭、布施與苦行時，總是由頌持『唵』開始的。

25.「心求解脫者在行獻祭、苦行或布施時，會以頌持『沓』（意思是『那』）開始，心中沒有果報之念。

26.「『薩』意指實相，也就是至善，而且阿朱納啊！它也是用來表示具有無比功德的行為。

27.「堅定於獻祭、苦行與布施也稱為『薩』，所以任何唯獨為上主而做的行動作為也同樣稱為『薩』。

19. Austerity done under delusion, and accompanied with sorcery or torture to oneself or another, may be assumed to spring from Ignorance.

20. The gift which is given without thought of recompense, in the belief that it ought to be made, in a fit place, at an opportune time and to a deserving person – such a gift is Pure.

21. That which is given for the sake of the results it will produce, or with the hope of recompense, or grudgingly – that may truly be said to be the outcome of Passion.

22. And that which is given at an unsuitable place or time or to one who is unworthy, or with disrespect or contempt - such a gift is the result of Ignorance.

23. Om, Tat, Sat is the triple designation of the Eternal Spirit, by which of old the Vedic scriptures, the ceremonials and the sacrifices were ordained.

24. Therefore all acts of sacrifice, gifts and austerities, prescribed by the scriptures, are always begun by those who understand the Spirit with the word Om.

25. Those who desire deliverance begin their acts of sacrifice, austerity or gift with the word Tat (meaning "That"), without thought of reward.

26. Sat means Reality or the highest Good, and also, O Arjuna! it is used to mean an action of exceptional merit.

27. Conviction in sacrifice, in austerity and in giving is also called Sat. So too an action done only for the Lord's sake.

28.「不論是獻祭、苦行、布施，或從事所有任何事宜，如果
　　是沒有信仰而為之，就稱之為『阿薩』（意指不真實），因
　　為那是『薩』的對立面。阿朱納啊！這樣的行為毫無意
　　義，不管是如今或未來。」[2]

這就是聖靈的科學與自我認識的藝術、奧義書之一的聖
典——《薄伽梵歌》中，克里希納與阿朱納王子對話的第十七
章，名為「信仰三別」。

2　梵文中，字首的「a」常代表否定，與英文相同。例如，himsa 在梵文中是傷害、暴力，
　　ahimsa 就是不傷害、無暴力。

28. Whatsoever is done without faith, whether it be sacrifice, austerity or gift or anything else, is called *asat* (meaning "unreal") – for it is the negation of S$_{AT}$, O Arjuna! Such an act has no significance, here or hereafter.

Thus, in the Holy Book the Bhagavad Gita, one of the Upanishads, in the Science of the Supreme Spirit, in the Art of Self-Knowledge, in the colloquy between the Divine Lord Shri Krishna and the Prince Arjuna, stands the seventeenth chapter, entitled: The Threefold Faith.

18

出離心
The Spirit of Renunciation

　　這場神聖的對話到這裡終於進入了尾聲。這一章從阿朱納詢問放棄與捨棄兩者的分別開始，而克里希納的回答則包含好幾個不同的主題，可說是為這整場對話做了總結。

　　克里希納一開始談論捨棄（renunciation，或譯出離，也就是桑雅薩〔sannyasa〕）與放棄（relinquishing; abandonment，也就是提雅嘎〔tyaga〕），兩者的差別。阿朱納之所以問這個問題，多少與印度的靈修傳統有關；因為傳統思維裡，傾向於認為修行者應像僧侶般放棄所有外在的一切。主的答覆是，真正的「放下」是內在的，也就是應以無執著與無所求之心行事。

　　克里希納接著依造化三性的不同，談論職責、內在的理智與信念，以及修行道路上的不同。例如，以知識、見解而言，純真者見到與眾生為「一」、沒有分別（18:20），熱情者見到與眾生為「異」、各不相同（18:21）；至於無明者，則只看到自己，沒有別人（18:22）。因此在理智上，純真者有明辨能力，熱情者分不清對錯，而無明者則以非為是（18:30-18:32）。

　　在這個對話的終尾，克里希納一再地向阿朱納保證：

「……你是我所摯愛的。」（18:64-18:65）

　　這其實也是主對我們的保證——彷如上主在我們耳邊輕聲地提醒——因為我們原本就是上帝的子女。最後，克里希納再一次提醒我們捨棄與臣服；善盡自己的職責，全心全意地專注於祂、敬拜祂，將所有一切身口意供養祂，如此我們就有了上主的最終保證。

1. 阿朱納問道：「偉大的主啊！我想知道放棄與捨棄有何不同？」

2. 克里希納答：「聖哲們說捨棄意味著棄絕所有源自欲望的行動作為；而放棄則是臣服於行動作為的結果（果報）。

3. 「一些哲學家說行為全然是邪惡的，都應捨棄。有些人則說獻祭、布施與苦行等行為不應捨棄。

4. 「印度之傑啊！且聆聽我對這個問題的判決。這個問題有三個面向。

5. 「獻祭、布施與苦行是當為而不應捨棄的，因為它們淨化了渴望的靈魂。

6. 「但當以無執著與無所求之心為之。這就是我的最終判決。

7. 「放棄義務所在的行為是不對的；如果誤解而置之不顧，那就全然是無明的結果。

8. 「若因畏懼身體受磨難可能帶來的痛苦而迴避行為，這就是依熱情而行事，所以捨棄的好處不會顯現。

9. 「履行義務，僅因為相信那是該盡的責任，沒有任何私人的欲望或冀求任何回報——這樣的捨棄就是出於純真。

Arjuna asked:

1. O Mighty One! I desire to know how relinquishing is distinguished from renunciation.

Lord Shri Krishna replied:

2. The sages say that renunciation means forgoing an action which springs from desire; and relinquishing means the surrender of its fruit.

3. Some philosophers say that all action is evil and should be abandoned. Others that acts of sacrifice, benevolence and austerity should not be given up.

4. O best of Indians! Listen to My judgment as regards this problem. It has a threefold aspect.

5. Acts of sacrifice, benevolence and austerity should not be given up, but should be performed; for they purify the aspiring soul.

6. But they should be done with detachment and without thought of recompense. This is My final judgment.

7. It is not right to give up actions which are obligatory; and if they are misunderstood and ignored, it is the result of sheer Ignorance.

8. To avoid an action through fear of physical suffering, because it is likely to be painful, is to act from Passion, and the benefit of renunciation will not follow.

9. He who performs an obligatory action, because he believes it to be a duty which ought to be done, without any personal desire either to do the act or to receive any return – such renunciation is Pure.

10.「臻至純真的智者，無有疑惑，擁有自我克制的精神，他們不會因行動所帶來的痛苦而退縮不前，也不會因行動所帶來的快樂而心存冀求。

11.「因為擁有肉身就無法完全迴避行動，因此以他們的情況而言，放棄行動的結果（果報）就可說是全然的捨棄。

12.「對無法捨棄所有欲望的人而言，行為的結果（果報）有三種：善，惡，或善惡兼具。但對於捨棄者，則無有果報。

13.「壯士啊！我現在將告訴你——根據哲學（數論）所揭示的——一項行動作為的發生完成，必須具備哪五種要素。

14.「這五項是：肉身（活動場所）、性格（行為者）、各種身體器官、它們的各種活動與命運。

15.「任何作為，不論是身、口或意，也不論是對或錯，這五項都是其基本肇因。

16.「但出於不成熟的判斷力，愚者認為全然是他自我一人所為，因而曲解真理，無法正確地看待事物。

17.「無有驕傲，且理智（智慧）無有染著，這樣的人儘管殺了人，但並不是真殺；他的作為不會束縛他。

10. The wise man who has attained purity, whose doubts are solved, who is filled with the spirit of self-abnegation, does not shrink from action because it brings pain, nor does he desire it because it brings pleasure.

11. But since those still in the body cannot entirely avoid action, in their case abandonment of the fruit of action is considered as complete renunciation.

12. For those who cannot renounce all desire, the fruit of action hereafter is threefold – good, evil, and partly good and partly evil. But for him who has renounced, there is none.

13. I will tell you now, O Mighty Man! the five causes which, according to the final decision of philosophy, must concur before an action can be accomplished.

14. They are a body, a personality, physical organs, their manifold activity and destiny.

15. Whatever action a man performs, whether by muscular effort or by speech or by thought, and whether it be right or wrong, these five are the essential causes.

16. But the fool who supposes, because of his immature judgment, that it is his own Self alone that acts, he perverts the truth and does not see rightly.

17. He who has no pride, and whose intellect is unalloyed by attachment, even though he kill these people, yet he does not kill them, and his act does not bind him.

18.「知識、知曉者與知識的對象,是引發行動作為的三元素;而行動(作為)、行動者(作為者)與工具三者,則是其組成要件。

19.「知識、行動與作為者因造化三性而各有歧異。且聽我道來:

20.「在所有眾生中見到不可毀滅的『一』、在個別的生命中見到無有分別的『一』,這樣的知識真可謂是純真的知識。

21.「認為形象各異的芸芸眾生為各自分別的生命──這樣的知識來自熱情。

22.「但盲目地執著於一想法,彷如其涵蓋一切,沒有邏輯思維,看不到真理,也沒有洞澈力,這種知識的根源是黑暗。

23.「依義務而為,無有私心與關心,無好亦無惡,亦不思慮其後果,這樣的行動是純真的。

24.「但即便在行動中付出最大的心力,如果作為者志在滿足其私欲,內在充斥著個人的虛榮,那麼這樣的行動可說是源自熱情。

25.「依妄念而為,既不在意其靈性意義,也不考量自身的能力或是行動可能帶來的傷害,這樣的行動可說是無明下的產物。

18. Knowledge, the knower and the object of knowledge, these are the threefold incentives to action; and the act, the actor and the instrument are the threefold constituents.

19. The knowledge, the act and the doer differ according to the Qualities. Listen to this too:

20. That knowledge which sees the One Indestructible in all beings, the One Indivisible in all separate lives, may be truly called Pure Knowledge.

21. The knowledge which thinks of the manifold existence in all beings as separate – that comes from Passion.

22. But that which clings blindly to one idea as if it were all, without logic, truth or insight, that has its origin in Darkness.

23. An obligatory action done by one who is disinterested, who neither likes it nor dislikes it, and gives no thought to the consequences that follow, such an action is Pure.

24. But even though an action involve the most strenuous endeavor, yet if the doer is seeking to gratify his desires, and is filled with personal vanity, it may be assumed to originate in Passion.

25. An action undertaken through delusion, and with no regard to the spiritual issues involved, or to the real capacity of the doer, or to the injury which may follow, such an act may be assumed to be the product of Ignorance.

26.「若人既無情緒也無個人虛榮之心，反而是擁有勇氣與信心，並且不在意成敗，那麼他的行為就是出於純真。

27.「衝動、貪婪、冀求回報、粗暴、不單純、心迴盪於悲喜之間，這樣的人的內在是為熱情所支配了。

28.「若此人優柔寡斷、卑鄙、頑固、不誠實、兇惡、懶惰、沮喪、拖延——這樣的人可說是在黑暗中。

29.「理智與信念也分三類，視造化三性何者主導而定。阿朱納啊！我將一一為你細說分明。

30.「了知生命的生與滅，知曉當為與不當為之分別，並能明辨畏與無畏、束縛與解脫——這樣的理智是純真的。

31.「分不清對錯，也不知當為與不當為之分別——這樣的理智是被熱情所掌控的。

32.「阿朱納啊！至於被無明所遮蔽的人，以非為是，顛倒看待事物——這樣的理智是由黑暗所統轄的。

33.「藉著信念與穩固的專注力，使得心念、維生系統（能）與感官都得以受到控制——阿朱納啊！這就是純真下的產物。

26. But when a man has no sentiment and no personal vanity, when he possesses courage and confidence, cares not whether he succeeds or fails, then his action arises from Purity.

27. In him who is impulsive, greedy, looking for reward, violent, impure, torn between joy and sorrow, it may be assumed that in him Passion is predominant.

28. While he whose purpose is infirm, who is low-minded, stubborn, dishonest, malicious, indolent, despondent, procrastinating – he may be assumed to be in Darkness.

29. Reason and conviction are threefold, according to the Quality which is dominant. I will explain them fully and severally, O Arjuna!

30. That intellect which understands the creation and dissolution of life, what actions should be done and what not, which discriminates between fear and fearlessness, bondage and deliverance, that is Pure.

31. The intellect which does not understand what is right and what is wrong, and what should be done and what not, is under the sway of Passion.

32. And that which, shrouded in Ignorance, thinks wrong right, and sees everything perversely, O Arjuna! that intellect is ruled by Darkness.

33. The conviction and steady concentration by which the mind, the vitality and the senses are controlled – O Arjuna! they are the product of Purity.

34.「總是牢牢地抓住儀式，看重自我的利益與財富，為的是後續能為自己帶來什麼──這樣的信念來自熱情。

35.「而倔強地執著於錯誤的理念、畏懼、悲傷、消沉與虛榮──這樣的信念是無明的產物。

36.「再聽聽三種不同的快樂。第一種是日益增加，解救人於悲慘中，

37.「一開始彷如毒藥，但後來卻猶如甘露──這樣的快樂是純真，因為它是自智慧而來的。

38.「另一種是使感官沉迷於感官對象中，所以一開始有如甘露，但終了卻像是毒藥──這樣的快樂來自熱情。

39.「至於那源自於懶惰、昏睡與愚蠢，自始至終只是在麻醉感官者──這樣的快樂出於無明。

40.「不論是此塵世或較高等世界的任一個角落，沒有任何事物可免於造化三性的影響──因為所有這些都生自於造化。

41.「阿朱納啊！不論是靈性導師（婆羅門）、軍士（剎帝利）、商賈（吠舍）或工人（首陀羅），他們的職責全部都是依其本性內主導的造化性質而訂定的。

34. The conviction which always holds fast to rituals, to self-interest and wealth, for the sake of what they may bring forth – that comes from Passion.

35. And that which clings perversely to false idealism, fear, grief, despair and vanity – it is the product of Ignorance.

36. Hear further the three kinds of pleasure. That which increases day after day delivers one from misery,

37. Which at first seems like poison but afterward acts like nectar – that pleasure is Pure, for it is born of Wisdom.

38. That which as first is like nectar, because the senses revel in their objects, but in the end acts like poison – that pleasure arises from Passion.

39. While the pleasure which from first to last merely drugs the senses, which springs from indolence, lethargy and folly – that pleasure flows from Ignorance.

40. There is nothing anywhere on earth or in the higher worlds which is free from the three Qualities – for they are born of Nature.

41. O Arjuna! The duties of the spiritual teachers, the soldiers, the traders and the servants have all been fixed according to the dominant Quality in their nature.

42.「平靜、自制、苦行、純淨、寬恕，以及正直、知識、智慧，與對上帝的信心——這些構成了靈性導師（婆羅門）的職責。

43.「英勇、榮耀、堅定、熟練、慷慨、臨戰不變，以及統轄有力——這些是軍士（剎帝利）的職責；它們由其本性而來。

44.「農作、保護牛隻與貿易是商賈（吠舍）的職責，同樣是依其本性而來。工人（首陀羅）的職責是服務，同樣也是與其本性一致。

45.「每個人只要勤奮地善盡其職守，就可證得圓滿。對於時時留意自己職責的人，如何可達到圓滿；且聽我為你述說。

46.「藉由將所有行為奉獻給上帝——祂是所有眾生的源頭，並且充滿所有的事物——人將可達至圓滿。

47.「盡自己的職責——不論是做得多不好，也總比去做別人的職責來得好，不論後者做得有多好。按照本性所揭示的去履行自己的職責，這樣的人永遠不會有罪業。

48.「儘管可能有所缺失，只要是屬於自己的職責就不應放棄。正如火焰會有煙霧遮蔽，所有的行動作為也都難免有缺憾。

42. Serenity, self-restraint, austerity, purity, forgiveness, as well as uprightness, knowledge, wisdom and faith in God – these constitute the duty of a spiritual Teacher.

43. Valor, glory, firmness, skill, generosity, steadiness in battle and ability to rule – these constitute the duty of a soldier. They flow from his own nature.

44. Agriculture, protection of the cow and trade are the duty of a trader; again in accordance with his nature. The duty of a servant is to serve, and that too agrees with his nature.

45. Perfection is attained when each attends diligently to his duty. Listen and I will tell you how it is attained by him who always minds his own duty.

46. Man reaches perfection by dedicating his actions to God, Who is the source of all being, and fills everything.

47. It is better to do one's own duty, however defective it may be, than to follow the duty of another, however well one may perform it. He who does his duty as his own nature reveals it, never sins.

48. The duty that of itself falls to one's lot should not be abandoned, though it may have its defects. All acts are marred by defects, as fire is obscured by smoke.

49.「全然無執著之心，戰勝自我，欲望也消除，如此之人藉由捨棄，臻至行為自行圓滿、無有留下業力種子的圓滿解脫之境界。

50.「我現在將簡短地說明臻至圓滿的人如何尋得永恆聖靈——也就是無上智慧的境界。

51.「總是由純然理智所指引，勇敢地節制自我，捨棄感官的對象，並且棄絕執著與憎恨；

52.「享受獨處、簡樸，身口意在完美的控制下，融入於靜坐沉思之中，這樣的人得到了解脫——總是充滿著捨棄之心。

53.「棄絕了自私、權力、傲慢、嗔怒與欲望，無擁有屬於自身之財物，並且內心達到了平安之境，這樣的人堪能加入永恆聖靈之行列。

54.「而當他與永恆合一，而且他的靈魂了知那來自於自性的恩典，他心中不再感到有欲望與悔悟，對所有眾生一視同仁，並且得享由獻身於我而來的無上恩典。

55.「藉著這樣的奉獻，他見到了我，認識了我，也瞭解了我；如是他了悟了真理，得以進入我的國度。

56.「所有的作為都依靠我，而且都是為我而作，藉著我的恩典，他證得了永恆不變的生命。

49. He whose mind is entirely detached, who has conquered himself, whose desires have vanished, by his renunciation, reaches that stage of perfect freedom where action completes itself and leaves no seed.

50. I will now state briefly how he, who has reached perfection, finds the Eternal Spirit, the state of Supreme Wisdom.

51. Guided always by pure reason, bravely restraining himself, renouncing the objects of sense, and giving up attachment and hatred;

52. ⌈Enjoying solitude, abstemious, his body, mind and speech under perfect control, absorbed in meditation, he becomes free – always filled with the spirit of renunciation.

53. Having abandoned selfishness, power, arrogance, anger and desire, possessing nothing of his own and having attained peace, he is fit to join the Eternal Spirit.

54. And when he becomes one with the Eternal, and his soul knows the bliss that belongs to the Self, he feels no desire and no regret, he regards all beings equally and enjoys the blessing of supreme devotion to Me.

55. By such devotion, he sees Me, who I am and what I am; and thus realizing the Truth, he enters My Kingdom.

56. Relying on Me in all his action and doing them for My sake, he attains, by My grace, Eternal and Unchangeable Life.

57.「因此在行動作為上臣服於我，安住於我之內，將理智專注於我，而且總是想著我。

58.「心念完全繫於我，如此因著我的恩典你將克服你道途上的障礙。但假如為驕慢所誤導，你將無法聆聽我的教誨，而且確然將會迷失。

59.「如若你因你的虛榮心而想逃避這個戰役，你也無法做到，因為造化必迫使你去做。

60.「阿朱納啊！你的職責束縛了你。它來自你的本性，而由於你的妄念，使你不願去做，但那卻正是你必須去做的。對此你無能為力。

61.「阿朱納啊！上帝住在所有眾生的心中，是祂的奧秘力量，使得眾生如在輪圈中輪迴往復。

62.「盡你所有的力量飛向祂，並且臣服於祂。藉著祂的恩典，你將證得無上平安之境、達至永生的住所。

63.「如是我已將真理——那奧秘中的奧秘——揭示予你。好好思量，你就可自由地如你所願去做。

64.「只是再聽我最後的一句話——那最深邃的秘密：你是我所摯愛的，你是我的朋友，而且我是為了你的福祉而說的。

57. Surrender then your actions unto Me, live in Me, concentrate your intellect on Me, and think always of Me.

58. Fix but your mind on Me, and by My grace you shall overcome the obstacles in your path. But if, misled by pride, you will not listen, then indeed you shall be lost.

59. If you in your vanity think of avoiding this fight, your will shall not be fulfilled, for Nature herself will compel you.

60. O Arjuna! Your duty binds you. From your own nature has it arisen, and that which in your delusion you desire not to do, that very thing you shall do. You are helpless.

61. God dwells in the hearts of all beings, O Arjuna! He causes them to revolve as it were on a wheel by His mystic power.

62. With all your strength, fly unto Him and surrender yourself, and by His grace shall you attain Supreme Peace and reach the Eternal Home.

63. Thus have I revealed to you the Truth, the Mystery of mysteries. Having thought over it, you are free to act as you will.

64. Only listen once more to My last word, the deepest secret of all; you are My beloved, you are My friend, and I speak for your welfare.

65.「獻身於我、敬拜我、將所有一切供養我、頂禮我,如此你必然會來到我這裡。我真正地向你保證;你是我所摯愛的。

66.「棄絕所有的俗世職責,唯獨臣服於我。不要焦慮;我將赦免你所有的罪業。

67.「對於沒有修持苦行的人,不能夠去愛,不願意聆聽,或對此嘲笑的人,不要將這些話語告訴他們。

68.「但對於將這個偉大奧秘教導於我的信眾的人,這就是最高的奉獻,而且他必然會來到我這裡。

69.「在眾人對我的服侍中,再沒有比這個更珍貴的了;而我對他的珍愛,在這世間也無人能及。

70.「研讀我們此一靈性對話的人,我向你保證,必然也會因此而在智慧的祭壇上向我禮拜。

71.「是的,只要以信心與無懷疑之心聆聽此教誨,他也能免於惡業,並提升自己到有道德者藉由德行所能達到的境界。

72.「阿朱納啊!你有專心聽我說的話語嗎?你的無明與妄念離去了嗎?」

73. 阿朱納答:「主啊!我的迷惑不再。永不變的主啊!藉著您的恩典,光明已現眼前,疑惑已離我遠去。而今我站在您面前,願遵您的旨意而行。」

65. Dedicate yourself to Me, worship Me, sacrifice all for Me, prostrate yourself before Me, and to Me you shall surely come. Truly do I pledge to you; you are My own beloved.

66. Give up then your earthly duties, surrender yourself to Me only. Do not be anxious; I will absolve you from all your sin.

67. Speak not this to one who has not practiced austerities, or to him who does not love, or who will not listen, or who mocks.

68. But he who teaches this great secret to My devotees, his is the highest devotion, and verily he shall come unto Me.

69. Nor is there among men any who can perform a service dearer to Me than this, or any man on earth more beloved by Me than he.

70. He who will study this spiritual discourse of ours, I assure you, he shall thereby worship Me at the altar of Wisdom.

71. Yea, he who listens to it with faith and without doubt, even he, freed from evil, shall rise to the worlds which the virtuous attain through righteous deeds.

72. O Arjuna! Have you listened attentively to My words? Have your ignorance and your delusion gone?

Arjuna replied:

73. My Lord! O Immutable One! My delusion has fled. By Your Grace, O Changeless One, the light has dawned. My doubts are gone, and I stand before You ready to do Your will.

74. 山佳亞道：我如是聆聽了上主師利克里希納與偉大靈魂阿朱納，兩人間這場希有、奇妙，而且又鼓舞心靈的對話。

75. 因著聖人毗耶娑的恩典，我得以由大師——上主師利克里希納——口中，聆聽到這神秘而又高貴的科學。

76. 國王啊！我越去思維那場奇妙而神聖的對話，我也就越加地在這喜悅之中渾然忘我。

77. 每當我一再地回憶起上主那非凡的美，我心中充滿了驚奇與幸福。

78. 我全全然然地確信，不論上主師利克里希納——智慧的王子——在哪裡，也不論偉大的射手阿朱納在哪裡，那裡就會有好運、勝利、幸福與正義。

這就是聖靈的科學與自我認識的藝術、奧義書之一的聖典——《薄伽梵歌》中，克里希納與阿朱納王子對話的第十八章，名為「出離心」。

願上主師利克里希納護佑加持你！

Sanjaya told:

74. Thus have I heard this rare, wonderful and soul-stirring discourse of the Lord Shri Krishna and the great-souled Arjuna.

75. Through the blessing of the sage Vyasa, I listened to this secret and noble science from the lips of its Master, the Lord Shri Krishna.

76. King! The more I think of that marvelous and holy discourse, the more I lose myself in joy.

77. As memory recalls again and again the exceeding beauty of the Lord, I am filled with amazement and happiness.

78. Wherever is the Lord Shri Krishna, the Prince of Wisdom, and wherever is Arjuna, the Great Archer, I am more than convinced that good fortune, victory, happiness and righteousness will follow.

Thus, in the Holy Book the Bhagavad Gita, one of the Upanishads, in the Science of the Supreme Spirit, in the Art of Self-Knowledge, in the colloquy between the Divine Lord Shri Krishna and the Prince Arjuna, stands the eighteenth chapter, entitled: The Spirit of Renunciation.

May the Lord Shri Krishna bless you!

主要人物對照表

Abhimanyu　　　激昂，阿朱納與妙賢之子。

Arjuna　　　阿朱納，也譯阿周那、阿尊拿，或有修。般
　　　　　度五子的第三子，為昆蒂與雷神因陀羅所生。

Bhima　　　怖軍，般度五子的第二子，為昆蒂與風神凡
　　　　　裕所生。

Bhishma　　　毗濕摩，恆河女神和福身王的兒子；是持國
　　　　　百子和般度五子的伯父。

Dhritarashtra　　持國，持國王。

Draupadi　　　德羅帕蒂，也譯為黑公主；般度五子的共同
　　　　　妻子。

Duryodhana　　難敵，持國王與王后甘陀利的持國百子中的
　　　　　長子。

Krishna　　　克里希納，也譯為黑天、奎師那。

Kunti　　　昆蒂，般度之妻，般度前三子之母。

Madri　　　瑪德利，般度之妻，般度後二子之母。

Nakula　　　無種，般度五子的第四子，為瑪德利與孿生
　　　　　雙神所生。

Sahadeva　　　偕天，般度五子的第五子，為瑪德利與孿生
　　　　　雙神所生。

Sanjaya　　　山佳亞，也譯為良知、全勝。

Vyāsa　　　廣博，也譯為廣博仙人、維亞薩、毗耶娑。

Yudishthira　　堅陣，堅陣王，般度五子的長子，為昆蒂與
　　　　　至尊神達摩所生。

專有名詞對照表

Absolute	絕對者、絕對之境；亦即上帝、上主
Apana	下行氣
attain	證得、達到
being	存在、存有、本質、生命
bhakti yoga	巴克提瑜伽、奉愛瑜伽、虔誠瑜伽、虔信瑜伽
Brahman	梵
Brahmana	婆羅門、僧侶
Brahmin	婆羅門、僧侶
Divine	至聖、神聖；亦即上帝
dhyana	禪那、禪、靜慮
eternal	永恆、不朽、永生
ignorance	無明、愚昧、惰性（inertia）
intellect	理智
jnana	闍那、知識
karma	羯磨、業障、行動
Lord	主、上主
meditation	靜坐、沉思、冥想、靜心、打坐
merit	功德、福報。福報（blessed rewards）與功德其實是不同的，前者是人天福報，後者才是帶往解脫；二者的分別在是否有「我」。但在此普羅希並沒有特別在用字上做區分。
mind	心、心智、心念、頭腦、意念、意
Nature	造化、大自然、自然
offering	供養
passion	熱情、情感、變性、激性

Prana	上行氣
Prakriti	普拉克里提；形塑心智與物質世界的基本能量或力量、造化、自然
purity	純潔、純真、悅性、善性
realization	了悟
renounce	捨棄
renunciation	捨棄
sacrifice	獻祭、犧牲奉獻、犧牲供養
self	小我
Self	自性、大我；印度教經典則稱之為「阿特曼」（aīman）
sin	罪業
Shri（Sri）	神聖之稱號，字義上相當於基督宗教的封聖（如聖約翰）
service	服侍、服事、服務
Supreme	至上、無上，指上帝
Supreme Self	無上聖靈，普羅希在他的英譯中，將「梵」譯為無上聖靈

參考文獻

尤煌傑，2001，《引頸企盼的思維者》，應用心理研究 9，87-114。

任繼愈，1987，《老子新譯》，谷風出版社。

江亦麗，2007，《恆河之魂：印度教漫談》，東大圖書公司。

印順法師，2004，《佛法概論》，正聞出版社。

林懷民譯，2008，《摩訶婆羅達》（譯自卡里耶爾法文劇本的英譯本），聯合文學出版社。

邱顯峯譯，2010，《薄伽梵歌》，喜悅之路靜坐協會。

陳師蘭與林許文二，2008，《印度聖境旅人書》，柿子文化。

鍾文秀譯，2011，《薄伽梵歌》，空庭書苑。

雪莉·雪莉·阿南達慕提，2008，《生命的真諦：薄伽梵歌》，阿南達瑪迦出版社。

張澄基，1973，《佛學今銓》，慧炬出版社。

黃晨淳編著，2004，《印度神話故事》，好讀出版社。

黃寶生譯，2005，《摩訶婆羅多：毗濕摩篇》，貓頭鷹出版社。

孫晶，2007，〈印度吠檀多哲學的梵我關與朱子理學之比較〉，第十屆儒佛會通暨文化哲學學術研討會。

鄔斯賓斯基，1954，《人可能進化的心理學》，楊斐華譯，斐華出版社。

鄔斯賓斯基，1984，《第四道》，楊斐華譯，斐華出版社。

鄔斯賓斯基，1999，《探索奇蹟》，黃承晃等譯，方智出版社。

楊斐華譯，1985，《薄伽梵歌》，斐華出版社。

蔣維喬、袁了凡，1998，《靜坐法輯要》，文津出版社。

懷塵譯，1999，《薄伽梵歌》，中國瑜伽出版社。

Cato, Molly Scott, 2010, *Green Economics: An Introduction to Theory, Policy and Practice*（中文版《綠色經濟學：理論、政策與實務》，周賓凰、徐耀南、王絹淑譯，智勝出版社）

Chatterjee, Satishchandra and Dhirendramohan Datta, 2012 *Indroduction to Indian Philosophy*（中文版《印度哲學概論》，伍先林、李登貴、黃彬等譯，黎明文化）

Easwaran, Eknath, 1985, *Bhagavad Gita*, Nilgiri Press.

Fosse, Lars Martin, 2007, *Bhagavad Gita*, YogaVidya.com LLC.

Kaminoff, Leslie, 2007（中文版《瑜伽解剖書》，謝維玲譯，大家出版社）

Seligman, Margin E. P., 1998, *Learned Optimism*（中文版《學習樂觀、樂觀學習》，洪蘭譯，遠流出版社）

Shattuck, Cybelle, 1999, *Hinduism*（中文版《印度教的世界》，楊玫寧譯，貓頭鷹出版社）

Shri Purohit Swami, 1935, *Bhagavad Gita*, http://www.thebigview.com/download/bhagavad-gita.pdf;（annotation by Kendra Crossen Burroughs, 2010, Skylight Paths Publishing.)

Smith, Huston, 1995, *The World's Religions*（中文版《世界宗教》，劉安雲譯，立緒出版社）

Sri Swami Sivananda, *Bhagavad Gita*, http://www.dlshq.org/download/bgita.pdf

Yogananda, Paramahansa, 1999, *The Bhagavad Gita: God talks with Arjuna*, 2nd edition, Self-Realization Fellowship.

國家圖書館出版品預行編目資料

薄伽梵歌（中英對照本）/ 毗耶娑(Vyāsa)作；周賓凰譯. -- 初版. -- 臺
　北市：啟示出版：家庭傳媒城邦分公司發行, 2018.09
　面；　公分. --(Knowledge系列；21)
中英對照
譯自：Bhagavad Gita

ISBN 978-986-96765-1-9（平裝）

1.印度哲學 2.瑜伽

137.84　　　　　　　　　　　　　　　　107013305

Knowledge系列21

薄伽梵歌

作　　　者／毗耶娑（Vyāsa）
譯　　　者／周賓凰
總　編　輯／彭之琬
責　任　編　輯／彭之琬
特　約　編　輯／鄭榮珍

版　　　權／黃淑敏、翁靜如
行　銷　業　務／王　瑜、林秀津
總　經　理／彭之琬
發　行　人／何飛鵬
事業群總經理／黃淑貞
法　律　顧　問／元禾法律事務所 王子文律師
出　　　版／啟示出版
　　　　　　臺北市 104 民生東路二段 141 號 9 樓
　　　　　　電話：(02) 25007008　傳真：(02)25007759
　　　　　　E-mail:bwp.service@cite.com.tw
發　　　行／英屬蓋曼群島商家庭傳媒股份有限公司城邦分公司
　　　　　　台北市中山區民生東路二段141號2樓
　　　　　　書虫客服服務專線：02-25007718；25007719
　　　　　　服務時間：週一至週五上午09:30-12:00；下午13:30-17:00
　　　　　　24小時傳真專線：02-25001990；25001991
　　　　　　劃撥帳號：19863813；戶名：書虫股份有限公司
　　　　　　讀者服務信箱：service@readingclub.com.tw
　　　　　　城邦讀書花園：www.cite.com.tw
香港發行所／城邦（香港）出版集團
　　　　　　香港九龍九龍城土瓜灣道86號順聯工業大廈6樓A室 E-mail: hkcite@biznetvigator.com
　　　　　　電話：(852) 25086231　傳真：(852) 25789337
馬新發行所／城邦（馬新）出版集團【Cite (M) Sdn Bhd】
　　　　　　41, Jalan Radin Anum, Bandar Baru Sri Petaling, 57000 Kuala Lumpur, Malaysia.
　　　　　　電話：(603) 90578822　傳真：(603) 90576622
　　　　　　Email: cite@cite.com.my

封　面　設　計／李東記
封　面　文　案／江信慧、楊逢財
排　　　版／極翔企業有限公司
印　　　刷／韋懋實業有限公司

■ 2018 年 9 月 4 日初版　　　　　　　　　　Printed in Taiwan
■ 2024 年 2 月 5 日初版 5 刷
定價 360 元

城邦讀書花園
www.cite.com.tw

廣　告　回　函
北區郵政管理登記證
北臺字第000791號
郵資已付，免貼郵票

104　台北市民生東路二段141號2樓

英屬蓋曼群島商家庭傳媒股份有限公司城邦分公司　收

- -

請沿虛線對摺，謝謝！

書號：1MC021　　書名：薄伽梵歌

讀 者 回 函 卡

感謝您購買我們出版的書籍！請費心填寫此回函卡，我們將不定期寄上城邦集團最新的出版訊息。

姓名：＿＿＿＿＿＿＿＿＿＿＿＿＿＿＿＿　性別：□男　□女

生日：西元＿＿＿＿＿＿年＿＿＿＿＿＿月＿＿＿＿＿＿日

地址：＿＿＿＿＿＿＿＿＿＿＿＿＿＿＿＿＿＿＿＿＿＿＿

聯絡電話：＿＿＿＿＿＿＿＿＿＿　傳真：＿＿＿＿＿＿＿

E-mail：

學歷：□ 1. 小學 □ 2. 國中 □ 3. 高中 □ 4. 大學 □ 5. 研究所以上

職業：□ 1. 學生 □ 2. 軍公教 □ 3. 服務 □ 4. 金融 □ 5. 製造 □ 6. 資訊

　　　□ 7. 傳播 □ 8. 自由業 □ 9. 農漁牧 □ 10. 家管 □ 11. 退休

　　　□ 12. 其他＿＿＿＿＿＿＿＿＿＿＿＿＿＿＿＿＿＿

您從何種方式得知本書消息？

　　　□ 1. 書店 □ 2. 網路 □ 3. 報紙 □ 4. 雜誌 □ 5. 廣播 □ 6. 電視

　　　□ 7. 親友推薦 □ 8. 其他＿＿＿＿＿＿＿＿＿＿＿＿

您通常以何種方式購書？

　　　□ 1. 書店 □ 2. 網路 □ 3. 傳真訂購 □ 4. 郵局劃撥 □ 5. 其他＿＿＿

您喜歡閱讀那些類別的書籍？

　　　□ 1. 財經商業 □ 2. 自然科學 □ 3. 歷史 □ 4. 法律 □ 5. 文學

　　　□ 6. 休閒旅遊 □ 7. 小說 □ 8. 人物傳記 □ 9. 生活、勵志 □ 10. 其他

對我們的建議：＿＿＿＿＿＿＿＿＿＿＿＿＿＿＿＿＿＿＿

＿＿＿＿＿＿＿＿＿＿＿＿＿＿＿＿＿＿＿＿＿＿＿＿＿＿

＿＿＿＿＿＿＿＿＿＿＿＿＿＿＿＿＿＿＿＿＿＿＿＿＿＿